If what you're currently doing would get you more of what you want, the more would have already showed up. This book will show you how to take the kind of bigger action that will finally produce the results you want. I highly recommend it!

—JACK CANFIELD, CO-AUTHOR OF THE CHICKEN SOUP FOR THE SOUL® SERIES AND THE SUCCESS PRINCIPLES™

Think Big Act Bigger rises above the excuses and encourages readers to put themselves out there and steamroll obstacles.

—PIERS MORGAN, BRITISH JOURNALIST, FORMER CNN HOST, NBC's THE CELEBRITY APPRENTICE WINNER

From out of the tank and into the fire, Hayzlett just turned up the heat with *Think Big Act Bigger*.

—DAYMOND JOHN, FOUNDER AND CEO OF FUBU, STAR OF ABC's SHARK TANK

Think Big Act Bigger cuts through the bullshit and reveals that there is no illusion to success!

—PENN JILLETTE, OF PENN & TELLER, MAGICIAN AND COMEDIAN

Drawing on his own experiences and observations, Jeffrey lays out an actionable plan for how to develop your own brand and story and combine attitude with action to succeed. Fun to read and valuable for anyone, whatever their professional interests.

—CHRISTIE HEFNER, CHAIRMAN OF HATCH BEAUTY, FORMER EXECUTIVE CHAIRMAN OF CANYON RANCH ENTERPRISES AND FORMER CHAIRMAN AND CEO OF PLAYBOY ENTERPRISES, INC.

This book is a great investment in yourself and an even better investment in your business.

—BARBARA CORCORAN, REAL ESTATE MOGUL, BUSINESS EXPERT, STAR OF ABC's SHARK TANK

Hayzlett was born to write this book: fearless, bold, and a little irrational.

—HARVEY MACKAY, NEW YORK TIMES BESTSELLING AUTHOR

Read this book and you will soak up more information than a ShamWow!

—KEVIN HARRINGTON, ENTREPRENEUR AND BUSINESS EXECUTIVE

If *Think Big Act Bigger* was a man or woman, it would be the strongest of them all.

—GREG GLASSMAN, CEO OF CROSSFIT

Give me Liberty or give me *Think Big Act Bigger*!

—JOHN HEWITT, CEO AND CHAIRMAN OF LIBERTY TAX

America runs on coffee, but great businesses run on thinking big and acting bigger.

—JOHN COSTELLO, PRESIDENT OF GLOBAL MARKETING AND INNOVATION FOR DUNKIN' BRANDS

Get your business cooking by reading *Think Big Act Bigger*.

—GJ HART, EXECUTIVE CHAIRMAN, CEO AND PRESIDENT OF CALIFORNIA PIZZA KITCHEN

Think Big Act Bigger runs races around the competition.

—ELLIOT WALDEN, PRESIDENT AND CEO OF RACING OPERATIONS FOR WINSTAR FARM, AND FORMER THOROUGHBRED RACEHORSE TRAINER

Read *Think Big Act Bigger* and level up your success in the game of life!

—NOLAN BUSHNELL, FOUNDER OF ATARI CORPORATION AND CHUCK E. CHEESE, TECHNOLOGY PIONEER, ENTREPRENEUR AND SCIENTIST

THINK BIG
ACT BIGGER

THE REWARDS OF BEING RELENTLESS

JEFFREY HAYZLETT
WITH JIM EBER

Ep
Entrepreneur
PRESS®

Entrepreneur Press, Publisher
Cover Design: Andrew Welyczko
Production and Composition: Eliot House Productions

This publication is designed to provide accurate and authoritative information
in regard to the subject matter covered. It is sold with the understanding that
the publisher is not engaged in rendering legal, accounting or other professional
services. If legal advice or other expert assistance is required, the services of a
competent professional person should be sought.

Library of Congress Cataloging-in-Publication Data
    Hayzlett, Jeffrey W.
        Think big, act bigger: the rewards of being relentless/by Jeffrey Hayzlett,
    with Jim Eber.
        pages cm.
        ISBN-13: 978-1-59918-574-3 (hardback)
        ISBN-10: 1-59918-574-1 (hardback)
        1. Management. 2. Leadership. 3. Strategic planning. 4. Success in business.
    I. Title.
        HD31.H39453 2015
        658.4'012—dc23   2015016854

Printed in the United States of America

19 18 17 16 15   10 9 8 7 6 5 4 3 2 1

CONTENTS

INTRODUCTION
"Because I can" IX

PART ONE
OWN IT!

CHAPTER ONE
Tell Bigger Stories: And Make Sure Everyone
Around You Does, Too 3

Be Yourself in Everything You Do. 4

Own Your Own Story 6

Your Way, Not the Highway 11

"The Katelyn Rule" 12

Lessons Learned: Tell Bigger Stories. 17

CHAPTER TWO

SAY IT: NO ONE IS GOING TO DIE! Passion Makes Perfect,
Not Perfection.. **19**
Fail Fast? I'd Rather Succeed Fast 21
No Matter What You Do, Sometimes Things Will Fail........ 23
Some of the Best Ideas Start with Someone
    Saying "Hey, Watch This!"................................. 25
Lessons Learned: No One Is Going to Die 28

CHAPTER THREE

BE WILLING TO BE A LITTLE PIGHEADED AND IRRATIONAL: Push Harder
and Farther Than You Have Before—No Excuses! **31**
Push Harder: Be a Little Pigheaded.......................... 32
Push Farther: Be a Little Irrational 34
Get a Little Crazy—Push a Rope!............................ 36
Own It! No Excuses!.. 39
Lessons Learned: Be a Little Pigheaded and Irrational........ 44

PART TWO

FOCUS IT!

CHAPTER FOUR

KILL THE SQUIRREL: Focus on What Matters **49**
Focus on the Right Squirrels 50
Focus on the Right Business................................. 56
Focus on the Right "Matter"................................. 61
Focus the Team on the Right Things........................ 62
Lessons Learned: Kill the Squirrel.......................... 64

CHAPTER FIVE

DEVELOP YOUR OWN FLOW: Cadence Matters! **67**
What's Your Cadence? 68
Let Your People Flow—From You! 72
Lessons Learned: Develop Your Own Flow.................. 75

CHAPTER SIX

Clean YOUR OWN BATHROOM: Stay Grounded and Connected **77**

Call Me Mr. Clean, Not Johnny Vegas 79

Show, Don't Tell 81

The Perils of Disconnection 83

The Dangers of Losing Perspective 87

Lessons Learned: Clean Your Own Bathroom 91

PART THREE

MAKE IT HAPPEN!

CHAPTER SEVEN

Steamroll OBSTACLES and Enemies: Think Differently! **95**

Your Way Can Be Drastically Different 99

Know the Power of "And" 103

Be Resilient 105

We Live in Stories and Every Good Story Needs a Villain..... 107

Lessons Learned: Obstacles and Enemies 110

CHAPTER EIGHT

Be in a Constant State of Awareness: Get Over Yourself
and Know What You Don't Know **113**

What It Means to Know What You Don't Know............. 116

Admitting You Suck 119

Can Down-and-Out Companies Get Their Mojo Back? 124

"The Truth Is Out There" 127

Lessons Learned: Know What You Don't Know 130

CHAPTER NINE

FIND a BIGGER POND: Always Ask, "What's Next?" **131**

What's Next: Find a Bigger Pond.......................... 133

Re-Envision the Pond: Adapt 135

Find New Ponds: Ask Directions—and Listen to the Answers .. 139

Move Faster in Your Pond: Automate and Systematize....... 143

Combine Ponds: Sell Up, Not Out 146

Lessons Learned: Find a Bigger Pond 149

CHAPTER TEN

Reach Out and Touch Someone: Have a Servant Mentality 151

Ask and Ye Shall Receive: The Promise
(and Pitfalls) of Ponies 154

A Servant Serves Others 157

Lessons Learned: Have a Servant Mentality 159

CONCLUSION

Get Off Your Ass and Make It Happen! 161

People and Companies Consulted 165

Acknowledgments 169

About the Author 171

Index 175

"Because I Can"

had been Chief Marketing Officer (CMO) at a Fortune 100 company for several years when I left to build my personal brand as a speaker, strategic business consultant, and media personality. I had spent my years as a CMO fighting against deep-seated "big company" limitations and was looking forward to getting back to the wide-eyed optimism, control, intimacy, and seemingly endless possibilities of being an entrepreneur. I wanted to build a dynamic, nimble business with just a small team that I could guide anywhere I wanted to go.

I wanted to build my brand first online, so I told my team, "Go find out what I need to do to boost my social media presence by 25,000 fans on

Facebook and Twitter as quickly as possible. Give me a plan for what I need to do, from increasing visibility to buying ads."

They came back to me and said they could get only 15,000 fans on each.

"Why?" I asked.

"Our budget."

"But I never *gave* you a budget! I just asked you to tell me *what it would take to get where we needed to go.*"

Silence.

[END SCENE. CUE CRICKETS.]

From my years as a successful small-businessman in printing, marketing, and business development in South Dakota, through my time as the CMO of that Fortune 100 company, and into my current work as a speaker, bestselling author, host of a national TV show, and creator of the C-Suite Network, people have asked me one question more than any other: "Jeff, how did you do it?" My answer is: "I think big and act bigger." I'm a cowboy from Sioux Falls who worked his way up through businesses small and large to win on the national level. In fact, I win all the time, and my ability to think big and act bigger has been the key to my success.

Napoleon Hill's classic book *Think and Grow Rich* has taught millions of us that thinking is the first step in achieving. But acting bigger is the key to achieving bigger. Acting bigger means tying visions to actions—getting beyond the stories and excuses, the self-imposed limitations, preconceived notions, and constraining structures—and becoming the biggest, baddest, best version of who you are and what you want to be. The most dangerous move in business is the failure to make a move that delivers on a promise to be that "you." The history of modern business is filled with companies that no longer exist because their leaders refused to adapt and change until it was too late. Kodak thought it was still in the film business and ignored its own proprietary work on the digital camera. BlackBerry thought its brand-named communication method could stem the need to innovate. Oldsmobile just got old with its customers, and when they started to die, so did the brand.

Most people seem to understand this on some level. So why do so many of us think small and act smaller? Why do so many smart entrepreneurs, business owners, managers, and leaders (not to mention parents and partners) fail to act bigger even when they think that way? Lots of reasons: They aren't sure what they really want; they aren't sure they can get what they really want; they are scared or doubtful and think that if they don't know how to get somewhere, it isn't going to happen; and, most important, they lack the right attitude to own who they are.

Thinking big and acting bigger is all about action and attitude: being fearless and bold, steamrolling obstacles, ignoring perceived limitations, and even being a little irrational and pigheaded at times. I've learned it is about being relentless in all I do but especially trusting in *who I am because I can.*

My attitude is always about owning who I am in everything I do: Sell me, sell the company; sell the company, sell me. When people hire me and say, "Make it like it used to be," I say, "No. You can't go back, and I don't want to." I don't look the way I did when I was 20; I look *better.* Sure, I have lost some hair, but I also lost any doubt as to who I am. I have gained some weight, but I have also gained experience, character, and worldliness that make me better than I ever have been. Simply put, I am all that I say you should be: fearless, bold, and relentless. That's not arrogance, that's awareness—that's an attitude that says, "I own who I am!"

All the things I will tell you in this book about thinking and acting big in all you do—leading, connecting, relating, focusing, adapting—are virtually meaningless if you don't know who you are. I don't care if you are a business of one or two people, an entrepreneur with devoted followers, or a leader at an established business. Maybe you are struggling to overcome ongoing obstacles. Maybe you are pushing to get to the next level and persuade your people to help you get there.

> *The key to thinking big and acting bigger for any person and any company of any age or size is to own who and what you are because you can.*

Maybe you are working in a rapidly growing business, trying to deliver on your brand promise and enact visions you believe in. Regardless of your business situation, it is essential that you know who you are and allow that understanding to guide your business.

It doesn't matter who or what you are, what your situation is, or what industry you're in, just like it didn't matter if I was in the mahogany boardroom of that Fortune 100 company or in the corner of my living-room startup; the limitations I faced exist everywhere. That's what I had missed that day when my team came back to me with their plans: I knew I could succeed, but that didn't automatically mean they did. Thinking big was one thing; acting big is another. Why do we let preconceived notions, structures, and differences prevent our businesses and us from delivering for the future? We must get ourselves *and* our people beyond the stories that limit us and learn new ones that expand our possibilities. Those old voices inside our heads give us every excuse in the world for *not* doing something. Breaking free from them is hard work that starts with three words: *because I can.*

Do *you* believe you can? That's the first of many essential questions you must ask to think big and act bigger. Asking these questions and telling new stories that lead to more possibilities, profit, and purpose-driven lives sounds so easy, right? So why do we keep falling into stories that lead in the opposite direction? Because those stories are *very powerful.* In fact, the easiest thing to do is to keep telling stories that shut us down, that absolve us of responsibility and accountability, that stifle innovation and investigation, that play it safe.

Think about the greatest athletes—not the superstars constantly in the spotlight with otherworldly skills, smarts, and strength, but the thousands of others who make up the teams they play on. They also believe they can win all the time, no matter how impossible it may seem. They believe in who they are. They don't just *think* they are better; they act bigger for themselves and for the team. That's what I do too—*because I can.*

Truth is, anyone can do this. If I can, you can, too. You can do it *because you can.* Not can't: *can.* Saying "I can't" is about excuses, not action—apathy, not attitude. Remember: Stories are powerful. We live for them every day. We look to them to inform the most mundane and important decisions we make, from the food we eat to the clothes we wear to the jobs we take, so we can feel good about our decisions. But what about *our* stories? We live *in* our stories, and yet we fail to see how they are holding us back. Let's attack and rewrite the stories that prevent us from owning who we are. Let's put new voices inside our heads that say, "I can think big, act bigger, and do it my way—*because I can.*"

PART ONE

OWN IT!

CHAPTER ONE

TELL BIGGER STORIES...

And Make Sure Everyone Around You Does, Too

The late comedian George Carlin had a stand-up bit in the 1970s called "Seven Words You Can Never Say on Television"—seven words he said were so inappropriate and offensive that the FCC had banned them from broadcast. Well, Carlin had nothing on me. Apparently, to one company at least, I was three times worse: It sent over a speaking contract with 21 words I could never say onstage.

Let me be clear: I have been known to drop f-bombs. I have cussed with aplomb and used language some might call "salty." I might even use such language in this book. Hide your children! Avert your eyes! Or just deal with it.

This company, an otherwise terrific software business, couldn't deal with it. They were willing to pay my speaking fee but wanted to fine me $500 for each time I used one of the words on the list, up to a total fine of $7,500. I counted on my fingers (math is not my strong suit) how many bad words that gave me: 15. Then I looked at the list. There were words on there I would never think of using. It would be very difficult for me to work them all in, but I *love* a challenge. I accepted the deal with every intention of using up all $7,500.

Forget for a moment that the company never discussed any of this with me before sending over these stipulations. (Want me to tone it down? Just ask me. Don't bring in the lawyers first.) What I couldn't figure out was why this company wanted me to speak in the first place if this is what they expected. I am an open book. No one hires a dog like me and wonders why he doesn't meow. I am not effective or for everyone, and I know it, but as a result, no one ever complains that they got something they were not expecting. Why would they want me to change who I was on a fundamental level? More to the point, why would anybody who has met me *expect* me to change?

My success comes from who I am, not from trophies or titles. When someone recently said to me, "You're wearing success well," I took it to mean that I'm wearing who I am at my core well. It's not the camera, the book, or the stage that gives me my authority and defines my success. It comes from the core of who I am and how I act every moment of the day. People sometimes tell me, "Jeff, I like that you're real. You really are who you are," and I always reply, "It's hard enough to be me. Why would I want to be someone else, too?"

> It all comes back to the core of who you are.

BE YOURSELF IN EVERYTHING YOU DO

I once saw a speaker ask on his Facebook page, "How do you become authentic?" I thought, "That has to be one of the craziest questions I have ever heard. Who were you before?" Being successful as a speaker, in business, and in life starts with authenticity; the most successful people I have known personally are (or were) the same at home as they were in the office. Steve Jobs was just as aggressive in his personal life as he was at Apple. My friend Daymond John, the founder of the multibillion-dollar FUBU clothing brand and one of the stars of *Shark Tank* on ABC, runs a slick business and lives a slick life; he literally and figuratively looks like, dresses like, and spends a million dollars all the time. Another Shark on *Shark Tank*, Barbara Corcoran, whose Corcoran Group is New York's largest real estate company, is as in-your-face in her personal life, in business, or on any show—hers or mine! And how refreshing. No one needs to second-guess them or their motives. You can trust them because they are the same people in every part of their lives.

Why have we all been so conditioned to think being our true selves at work is risky? That we need to be different people personally and professionally? That doesn't just sound inauthentic, it sounds *exhausting*. If you don't know who the hell you are, how the hell can you be someone? If you're not real, how can you expect to get real responses back from your team and your customers? How can you or your business stand for something?

> Anyone who makes you think you can't be yourself and be successful is selling you a lie—because it is not your story.

Yes, your story will need to evolve over time. Yes, you must refine how you think and act to face emerging challenges as you grow and face new competition. Yes, you have to adapt to respond to change. But if you do all this having defined the core of who you are and hold true to it in all parts of your life, evolution, refinement, and adaptations do not change who you are, only how and what you do. In my first book, *The Mirror Test*, I talked about how I am transparent about this 24/7: Sell me, sell the company; sell the company, sell me. I don't see the difference, and neither should you. Just like you can't be one person in your personal life and another in business, you can't separate who you are from what you do. The people who work with you are like a family, too, and you probably spend more time with them than you do your biological family. They need to see the real you, too.

"Not being you" might succeed in the short run, but over time, it will kill your *and* your team's morale, productivity, loyalty, vision, and eventually your bottom line. As soon as I began to understand this, business (and life) got a lot better and easier for me. So why do so many businesspeople not understand this? Some of them lack confidence. Some of them are afraid. But most of the time, they and their businesses are stuck in stories that say, "I can't."

Understanding what that means and taking the steps to break free is essential to thinking big, acting bigger, and being a bigger you by developing a "because I can" attitude.

OWN YOUR OWN STORY

After I gave a presentation to the National Speakers Association, several members asked me where my TED Talk was. I told them, "I will *never* do a TED Talk." They were stunned, but my reasons are clear.

If you have never clicked on the phenomenally popular TED Talks channel on YouTube, attended an event, or listened to the podcast or radio show, the presentations are a spin-off of the annual TED (Technology, Entertainment, Design) Conference, which attracts some of the most important people in the world to speak on topics from science to culture. TED Talks are videos up to 18 minutes long, which are created not only from the main conference but also numerous worldwide satellite events and can be on any topic. According to the TED website: "TED looks for engaging, charismatic speakers whose talks expose new ideas that are supported by concrete evidence and are relevant to a broad, international audience." Those talks have populated the web and social media like rabbits the past few years, and that leads into my two main problems with them.

First, I wasn't saying those members who asked me about my nonexistent TED Talk shouldn't do their own or that they can't lead to success, only that they weren't necessary. The world doesn't need another TED Talk to tell us what we have to do. I once heard someone say "TED Talks suck," and I am inclined to agree. TED speakers are often wonderful, inspirational, and entertaining, but the idolatry of TED has often led to too much change in the wrong direction—away from helping people become a bigger "you" and toward helping people do things the way the speakers tell them to. But there is no single solution to any problem—no one-size-fits-all approach, no absolute rule. Absolute rule is what makes totalitarian regimes tick. Think I'm going too far? Perhaps, but given our culture's propensity for quick sound bites and selective listening, it is a legitimate concern that has even led to parody via a hysterical quiz by MotherJones.com: "North Korean Slogan or TED Talk Sound Bite?" (www.motherjones.com/media/2015/02/quiz-north-korean-slogan-ted-talk).

My second problem with TED Talks ties into my larger problem with franchises and chain stores and what they have done to the American landscape (and mind). Don't get me wrong: I am a franchising fan, and I have no problem with convenience. But they provide an easy excuse to give up on individuality. When I go to Atlanta or Orlando or Houston or virtually any city across the United States, I can't tell one neighborhood from another; so many are filled with the usual sets of repeating and repeatable stores and houses. The founders of those stores may have been big thinkers who acted big, but the result of their work is sameness for the rest of us to buy into. TED Talks force people down the same path to imitation—to become a bigger "them," not a bigger "you." They say, "You must be like this!"

Am I saying I have never watched or even enjoyed a TED Talk? Of course not. I also enjoy a riblet appetizer at Applebee's occasionally. But I go out of my way to enjoy Stroud's chicken in Kansas City or bacon at Ben & Jack's Steak House when I return to my apartment in New York City. I support all the family-owned diners and neighborhood joints I can, because I like places with real people who have succeeded on their own terms. These people embrace the independence that comes with thinking big and acting bigger every single day.

So when I say, "Own it," I do *not* mean I want you to own who I am. I want you to own who *you* are. This is not a "be like me" book but a "learn to act like me but be yourself" book to become a bigger *you*. Everyone is inundated with lessons on exactly how to do something. I just want to inspire you to do something *as you*. I will never, ever tell you there is "One Truth." That's Jim Jones, not Jeffrey Hayzlett. I hope none of you are using this book to brew my Kool-Aid. Brew your own, with any flavor or color you want. Better yet, brew your own brand. Someone already came up with Kool-Aid; come up with your own drink. You are that good.

So, when I hear speaking consultants say, "You need to present things this way. You need to sell products in the back of the room. You need to have a training video." I say, "No, you don't. Not if you don't want to." They'll respond, "You can make a fortune doing it," and I'll say, "Yeah, I can make money, but I don't want to do it. And if I don't want to, I don't have to. Anyone who tells you otherwise is selling something they have a stake in."

I know this, because I once listened to those consultants who said I had to do things a certain way to be successful. I spent tens of thousands of dollars to position myself the right way, because that's how people told me others had done it. I had the pictures taken, like everyone else. I created marketing materials like everyone else. I bought the clothes like everyone else. I even ditched my cowboy boots! But I soon stopped doing things "their" way. *Because it was not me.* Can a speaking sizzle reel or a brochure be helpful? Yes, but you don't have to do any of this, and you cannot do it before you tap into your core. That's why when a person tells me, "I have to license my content online as the first step to success as a speaker," it feels like someone sticking needles in my ears. I want to grab them by the shoulders, like I wish someone had for me, and say:

> *Use who you are. OWN THAT.*

When someone says you must do this or that to be successful, tell those people to shut up; you're writing your own story. Why have something that looks like someone else when it could be you?

That's what your business needs to reflect, too: an identity of its own. Stop listening to "them" if you want to be the best you. The first time I did TV, I thought, "I have to act like more of a TV person," because that's what "they" said. All that did was make for bad TV, while just working on being the best version of me made for great TV. Consultants, speakers, masterminds . . . they always talk about secrets to success, but those "secrets" are really just about figuring out:

- Who are you?
- What do you want to do?
- Where do you want to go?
- What is your end game?
- How does all this connect to the story that sells you?

Tell me: What are your main criteria for the direction you want to go, your conditions of satisfaction that apply to all these questions? Can you list yours? If you can't, what the hell do you own? Someone else's expectations? Nothing at all? Mine have been the same for decades, and they always remind me why I'm in it at all. Everything I do in business has to meet these conditions of satisfaction: have the ability to make me money, to grow professionally, and to have fun doing it. Those are the criteria I use for any direction I want to go. I might consider a business opportunity that satisfies two of the three under the right circumstances, but never just one, no matter how good the money is. Yet none of my conditions do me any good if I can't use the conviction they give me to inform my story and thus connect them to what I am selling to an audience, my customers, my potential clients or business partners, and my teams. Start by finding out what makes you happy and meets your own conditions of satisfaction. Stop reading and do it now, because I have learned that every time I violate my conditions—every time I do something that won't build me wealth, make me grow, or be fun—it never works out and usually ends up costing me money.

Now, what are you *actually* selling? Selling is not a dirty word. We are all selling something. But what we must sell in the best way possible is bigger stories that connect on a deeper level to the product, person, or service. We are selling someone bigger ideas through us that connect to what they want! We talk a lot about getting your two- or three-sentence elevator pitch down for your business. That's essential, but how much work do you do on the story that goes with the pitch? Not the product or service alone, but the story that goes with it. Sometimes we *think* we know what we are selling, but we don't. In my first two books, I called this pitch the "118"—the number of seconds you actually have to pitch: eight seconds to hook people and no more than 110 seconds to reel them in. I still believe you need to hook people in eight seconds. That's the length of time it takes for someone to start losing attention and for a qualified ride in professional bull riding; you must get business prospects to lean in *and* hold their attention and not let them throw you off just like you were riding a bull. The next 110 seconds—and probably fewer—are the time to drive your message home with no bull. Audiences and readers love the idea of the "118," yet I am still surprised by how bad so many of them are at doing it. And I think I know an essential missing piece: They lack the connection to a deeper story.

I was speaking with the executives of MGM long before they appeared on my TV show, and they kept telling me they were in the gaming and hospitality businesses. I said, "No, that is your industry. You are in the experience business. I'm not coming to you just to gamble, drink, eat, see a show, and look out at the lights of the strip from my room. I'm coming for the experience as a whole. I'm coming for an experience that I think can get no better at any other place." If MGM's leadership looks at it like that, they can say, "How do I make the experience spectacular?"

For example, think about it like this: Domino's isn't selling pizza; it's selling ease and convenience for hungry students, busy parents, and tired workers. Those old AT&T commercials from the 1980s that told you to "Reach out and touch someone"? That wasn't about long-distance service; it was about connection. That's what Apple is selling today—not phones but status and social connection.

In the end, my way is always going to be right for me because it is mine: I'm writing my own story with purpose and direction and doing what I do because I can. I've gone from doing right and wrong on Main Street in Sioux Falls to right and wrong on Fifth Avenue in New York City and countless streets around the world. The only thing that ever limited me was the voices in my head telling me I couldn't be that or that I needed to do something different.

YOUR WAY, NOT THE HIGHWAY

Even when I met my conditions of satisfaction and owned my story, could I have done things differently or even better? Yes. But I'm doing it my way because I can. People sometimes call me arrogant for saying this. Would you prefer modesty? Modesty is for reflection, not action. Athletes might be humble in the public eye after the big win, but I assure you none of them went on that field anything less than arrogant, believing that they could win. That doesn't mean they didn't look, listen, and pay attention beforehand. It doesn't mean they don't care about the team, the coaches, or the fans. It doesn't mean they're assholes—the greatest ones never are. They just own who they are and what they have to do.

That's how you need to be in your business. Don't apologize for it or try to change who you are! Whenever Jim, my writer, hears about someone who tried to change who they were rather than be themselves, he tells the joke about the golden screw. A boy is born with a screw where his belly button should be. He goes through life questioning it, wondering why he is different from everyone else, longing to be rid of the golden screw. Finally, he consults a wise man who tells him to accept himself as he is rather than change to be someone else. The boy doesn't like the answer, so the wise man says, "Fine. Then on your next birthday, just unscrew it." The boy thanks him, and when he wakes up on his birthday, he gets a screwdriver, removes the screw, and his ass falls off.

I may be an ass sometimes, but I assure you that mine is firmly secured to who I am. Why would anyone want to act any other way? Too often we just don't believe that being ourselves and holding ourselves accountable must be foremost in everything we do. I have found who I am, own it, and am contented with it. I will never turn that screw, and neither should you.

Well, that's not entirely true. Sometimes I've turned the screw "because I can," fully aware my ass might fall off. I've refused high-paying jobs that would make me less happy. I've turned down daily hosting on national TV, because it wasn't what I wanted. I have taken on too many jobs because I saw my conditions of satisfaction in them all, and when my partners told me that I was doing too much I got pissed off. They will tell you they had to fight to make me see that, but I owned my mistake: I started because I can, and I stopped because I can.

In other words, I am always in control. Isn't that what all the companies selling technology to control our lives and our homes tell us? Everything connects through us, thus our responsibility is greater than ever to own the power of that connection. I'm not saying you shouldn't ask for advice, but at some point those voices just make you smaller.

> *Just stop and act: Make the voices in your head smaller, not you.*

I love how Tania Yuki, the brilliant young CEO of the social media company Shareablee, puts it: "I have to learn over and over to pull the trigger—to say 'I don't know the perfect answer. I don't know how to really start to do it. I am just going to do it.' Sure, crap comes to you every day that you have no idea how to deal with. You could collect the advice of great people all day long. I used to. I would reach out to five people I respected, and each one of them said something completely reasonable, good, and *different*. 'Mother of . . . What do I do now?' I thought. 'I guess I am just going to have to be me and decide what I think and own it.'"

Right! In the end, acting like you *can* make up for a lot of knowledge. Believing there is one right way or that absolute rules exist distracts us from seeing opportunities in different guises and being ready to act on them. Rules should be questioned, tested, reviewed over time, and broken if they are not a law or commandment. That is the single biggest difference between me and most other people. Imagine what you could accomplish by just being yourself and unapologetically owning your story. Be your story, live your story—that's the first key to unlocking your success.

"THE KATELYN RULE"

No matter what anyone says, there are ways to get things done without compromising who you are. And you want your people to be empowered in the same way—to act like themselves, but *bigger*. This is the foundation of what everyone in my office calls "The Katelyn Rule":

> *If I have to answer something or do something that you should be able to answer or do yourself, then why do I need you?*

Here's how the rule got its name.

From time to time, I am asked to consult for high-growth companies—businesses I call "Big Dogs." We love Big Dogs. Big Dogs are the cornerstone of our motto at The Hayzlett Group's TallGrass Public Relations: "To run with the big dogs, you got to learn to piss in the tall grass." I have a team that backs me up for these Big Dog consultations, and our work begins before we get the business. The team assembles background information and presentations, sits in on meetings, takes notes, and helps me do the deep dive into the work that needs to be done. As part of the companies' evaluation of us, we then meet with CEOs and their teams to lay out our plan and define what our value proposition is in light of what they have to pay us. We call this our "Big Dog Plan."

My team is all about being Big Dogs in the Big Dog Plan presentations: Do it big or go home. Expectations are high, which they were for the 2:00 P.M. presentation the day our newest employee, Katelyn (we'll call her that because that's her name), walked into my office about 15 minutes before we had to leave. In her hand was the single color copy of that day's Big Dog Plan presentation.

"Should I bring color copies of our presentation to the meeting?" she asked me.

Before I continue, let me tell you how Katelyn became part of our team. A little more than a month before this moment, I had given a talk to a large group of college students considering advertising as a profession. Like most events, the advertising group that invited me had started social media activation in the weeks before, and one woman was doing it consistently and smartly, not in a heavy-handed way: Katelyn.

> *Act like yourself, only bigger— remember The Katelyn Rule!*

That gets the attention of someone like me. I am always looking for talent when I work. I'm like a jumpy prairie dog sticking its head out of its hole looking for connections and danger: *Hey, what's going on? Who's here? Where's the eagle?*

Katelyn had impressed me. So, after my talk, I asked the audience who and where Katelyn was. I found her in the back row. "That young woman is going to go places," I told the entire audience. "She was the only one actively engaged on social media before this event, and I want to meet her." I asked her to come to the front where she belonged. When she got there, I shook her hand and said, "You're all getting a copy of my book today, but Katelyn is getting hers first." Later that day, I talked with Katelyn, told her she should come work for us, and made it happen.

And now Katelyn—the woman who was going places—had gone someplace she never should have: into my office, 15 minutes before a Big Dog Plan presentation, asking *me* if we needed color copies of that presentation. I swiveled my chair to face her. She's petite, so I was pretty much looking at her eye to eye.

"Katelyn, you are fairly new," I said. "You and I haven't really had a chance to talk much about expectations and promises. So here is what we are going to do: Let's imagine that you only get to ask me 21 questions a month. Why 21? I don't know, but let's imagine you get only 21 questions. They can be about anything. You can ask me about the meaning of life. You can ask me the difference between a steer and a bull. You can ask me about the best Italian restaurant in New York City. You can ask me if I think your boyfriend will like something you bought him. And, of course, you can ask me questions about work. Anything you can imagine, but you get only 21 questions. . . . Are you still going to ask me right now if we should take color copies to a meeting that we've been preparing for since you started? Is that one of your effing questions? Do you *really* want to use one of your questions right now?"

She took a breath. "Probably not."

"Good career move. Because if I have to answer that question, what the hell do I need you for?"

I could see my words start to sink in, so I continued: "This is what

I pay you for. This is what I expect from you. I hired you because you're going to be a superstar in this company, and I have to answer a question like that? What, are you nuts? That is not a Big Dog question. That is a question that no one with any experience should ask."

I paused to catch my breath. "Now, will we look better if we bring color copies instead of black and white?"

"Yes."

"Of course we will. Will anyone die if it is in black and white?"

"No."

"So, it is adequate."

"Yes, it is adequate."

"Now let me ask you a question. Let's imagine that I answered your question, 'Yes, we must and should print color copies because that's what Big Dogs would do.' Do you have time to make them before we go?"

"No."

"No. So why would you want me to say yes and then not have the ability to deliver?"

I looked at her. She looked at me, and it became clear that Katelyn now owned the rule that bears her name: If I have to answer something or do something that you should be able to answer or do yourself, then why do I need you? In fact, Katelyn never violated her namesake rule again. She is now a superstar. That's the reason the rule is named *in her honor*—

Empower your team to create and own what they do in support of everything you and your business do.

not because she continued to fail. In fact, her mistake helped me define my expectations for any team:

> *The people who work for you need to be empowered to create and own what they do in support of you, your team, and your customers or clients.*

Otherwise what do we need them for? If I am going to *own it*, my team needs to own it too and know:

> ➤ They must think things through and first ask themselves the questions they want to ask me.

- They are empowered to make decisions, because that's what I pay them for.
- Moments like these allow them to break free from limitations and lead to new stories, bigger thinking and action, and their own "because I can" attitudes.

Would this have happened with Katelyn even if I had explained my expectations before we had this encounter? That's a fair question, and the answer is, "Probably."

Just like the budget story from the introduction, I am constantly amazed at the self-imposed barriers smart, capable, willing, and especially young people put up for themselves. It's like an invisible force field around their bodies. But it's all in their heads. Who said they couldn't do that? Who put up those barriers? I hate to watch people miss out because of voices in their heads that say they can't. Few things make me angrier. If there were some magic bullets for eliminating whatever holds young people like Katelyn down rather than pushing them to be bigger than they are, I'd be the first to fire (and I'm a pretty good shot). All I can do is my part: Make sure I don't beat them down. You shouldn't, either.

And don't get me started about the youth of today being entitled and lazy and blah, blah, blah. There are issues with "us" as much as there are issues with "them." More often than not, the issue boils down to the fact that we want "them" to own our stories instead of learning, understanding, letting them create their own stories, and figuring out together how their stories fit in with ours. This is, at best, limiting if we know our stories and, at worst, downright awful if we don't.

Make sure your people know what your story is and understand their stories, too. Give your teams the tools to succeed, make sure they understand what you expect, and then let them put their stamp on it so they work hard and own it to win. Without that, you can only expect them to own your story, not theirs.

What's the problem with that? Richard Lowe, the president and chief operating officer of Franchise Services, Inc., which owns the brands Sir Speedy, PIP, Signal Graphics, and TeamLogic IT, explains it this way: "We give our franchisees everything they need to succeed: high-value products to sell and training in operations, production, finance, marketing, and sales. Yet the business is still theirs. They have to do the work and follow the system. Running one's own business still takes an entrepreneurial spirit and drive. It's a myth that people who own a franchise will be successful just because it is a franchise. We may give them the tools, but they have to be the driving force in their business."

"If you look at our most successful franchisees, you will see a common thread in the way they run their businesses and in their personalities," adds Don Lowe, Richard's father and the CEO of the company. "They recognize that they have a proven system to follow, take charge of their business, and make it work for them."

LESSONS LEARNED: TELL BIGGER STORIES

Remember: Stories are powerful. We live *for* and *in* them every day. As much as these stories give us the power to connect, we fail to see how they hold us back. Too many of us are stuck in stories that say, "I can't." We must replace those stories that prevent us from pushing forward and owning what we do—and especially who we are. If you don't know who the hell you are, how can you tell a story that sells you and connect it to something bigger? If you're not real, how can you expect to get real results and responses back from your team and your customers? How can you or your business stand for something? We must be the same authentic and genuine person in every part of our lives 24 hours a day.

- → Own your story and be yourself in everything you do, and you'll be successful as yourself, not telling a story that is essentially a lie.
- → When someone says you must do this or that to be successful, tell those people to shut up: You're writing your own story.
- → If you have to answer something or do something that your team should be able to answer or do themselves, then why do you need them?

➤ Empower your people to create and own their stories; share yours; and understand how those stories fit together to support you, your teams, and your customers.

The point is not to get the people who work with and for us to own our stories but for our people to learn, understand, and create their own stories and fit them in with ours. Having mutually compatible, complementary, and diverse stories that serve the interests of your business and its goals allows our people to take the tools we give them, engage the work, and own what they do to win—as themselves.

CHAPTER TWO

Say It: No One Is Going To Die!

Passion Makes Perfect, Not Perfection

Years ago, my family went to a wedding in Fargo, which at the time was a big deal for us. It was a brilliant day, and we were all feeling good walking down the busy main street when my wife, Tami, hit a crack in the sidewalk and face planted for all to see. A small crowd surrounded us as we helped her up. Mortified but largely unscathed, Tami said what so many of us do as she started walking again: "I just want to die."

"That's okay, Mom," my daughter, Lindsey, smiled. "I do it all the time."

We all do. Of course, Tami didn't really feel like dying. No one should. Sure, when we face plant publicly, we feel like idiots. How big an idiot and how much it hurts are directly proportional to the number of people who see us. Tami did feel like hiding, but no one should be embarrassed about the mistakes we make or the actions we take, even when we fall on our faces. We should own them because no one is going to die.

You've already heard me use a version of this expression in discussing The Katelyn Rule. In fact, I first wrote about having a "no one is going to die" attitude in my second book, *Running the Gauntlet*. "Repeat after me," I wrote. "No one is going to die from the changes you make in business. Say it: 'No. One. Is. Going. To. Die.'" Since then, I have refined the idea in speeches and presentations, but it still boils down to this: Nothing is ever going to be perfect. You're going to screw up. Things are going to not work. They might suck. You could even fail. *So what?* No one is going to die.

I remember hearing about Carl Bass, the CEO of the multinational software company Autodesk, telling analysts on one of his quarterly calls that the company's latest results were "an unmitigated disaster." He owned that his company fell on its face with *everyone* watching and . . . no one died. It was just a loss. Winners in sports, business, and life always know this. Tom Brady won his fourth Super Bowl as the quarterback of the New England Patriots in 2015, but he had a rocky start to his season. The media speculated about his "demise" after a sound thumping by Kansas City in week four. The next week, after a season-turning win over Cincinnati, he was asked if he was aware of the reports of his death. "The emails I get from people that are always so concerned, and I'm always emailing them back, telling them: 'Nobody died or anything. It's just a loss.'"

Like Brady, we often use some version of "no one is going to die" as a way to say, "Calm down. We have a plan. Losses may hurt, but they don't kill us. We will recover." In a July 2014 interview with a *New York Times Magazine* writer, Brady used the word "grieving"—a word we associate with dying—to describe the feeling of losing in the postseason, but he obviously knew his career was not dead. He kept thinking big and acting bigger the following season until he made it back to the Super Bowl and won. Playing on Brady's words, I prefer to use "no one is going to die" as an exhortation before the fact.

Sure, you will lose a few times. Heck, I often fail five to six times trying to launch something new. But if I wait for something perfect, I am still going to fail *and* miss new opportunities and possibilities. Thus, I exhort you to do what I do:

Connect your "no one is going to die" attitude to your success, not just your failures, and let it drive your passion as you think big and act bigger.

> *Get over yourself and move! What's it going to cost you not to own it and act?*

FAIL FAST? I'D RATHER SUCCEED FAST

"Fail fast!" "Pivot!" An entire business vocabulary has sprung up around the idea of failure. Talking about failure has become so en vogue it's even passé in some industries: A once-successful Silicon Valley conference called FailCon, well, *failed*. FailCon focused on presenters and attendees sharing stories of their flops, but the event's founder cancelled the 2014 conference because, as she told *The New York Times*, "Failure chatter is now so pervasive in Silicon Valley that a conference almost seems superfluous. It's in the lexicon that you're going to fail."

Going to fail? Really? Simply put, I'm with Captain Kirk from *Star Trek*: I may make mistakes, but I refuse to accept the parameters of the "Kobayashi Maru" or the no-win scenario as an assessment of my character. I get the moral dilemma behind tests like the one I saw people take on National Geographic Channel's *Brain Games*: A runaway train heading down a track will kill a bunch of bystanders unless you pull a switch and change the direction of the train, but pulling the switch will kill a single worker on the tracks: What do you do? I know this and countless other tests are about assessing my character and moral compass, but they are *ridiculous*. I understand the dilemma, but I don't accept the value of the no-win situation.

Simply put, failure has become too much of a badge of honor in this country. I'm never going into a situation thinking I'm going to fail no matter how risky or seemingly impossible it is. There is always a win-win scenario that doesn't involve hurting anyone if that's what you want to do. I get why we think it's okay to fail. Some companies file

Chapter 11 without shame and recover. It's a mechanism for a do over, and there is nothing wrong with a mulligan. But it's better *not* to use it.

I believe we are making so much of our mistakes and thinking of failure as the new black that we are getting bad at celebrating actual success. And isn't that what we are really talking about here: success? Did you ever notice in the stories about failures that we never talk to the long-term losers—only those who failed after making big wins or went on to greater triumphs? If they hadn't ever succeeded we wouldn't be talking to them. I wouldn't want to make a career as a continual loser who finds success only in failure. You wouldn't want to listen to me. No one listens to permanent losers.

Maybe the reason we don't celebrate success enough is because we think and act small; the successes are not much to celebrate. That's the real danger here: allowing the voices in our heads to creep in again and keep us from thinking and acting big.

> *Stop overthinking things, coming up with reasons why not, and then playing it safe.*

Here's the thing: How many of you believe that if faced with that *Brain Games* train test you could actually act? It's easy to answer hypothetical questions about morality, but these tests assume that we have the ability to act in the moment. I know too many people who would simply fail to act—not because they are bad people but because, as we hear in so many wartime stories, the stress of having to make that decision causes them to freeze. Few of us will ever face anything like the "Kobayashi Maru" or a runaway train, but one thing these scenarios prove is that the worst thing to do is nothing. Then *someone* dies no matter what, and no one even tried to act bigger. When no one is willing to act, no one fails, but no one wins either. NO ONE WINS.

We shouldn't celebrate failure, but we can't afford to wish it away. Sadly, this seems to be what we are teaching our kids: that everyone is a winner. After all, if everyone is a winner, then no one is. Why are we afraid of that? Whose self-esteem are we trying to protect: the parents' or the kids'? Take it from Michael Williams, the former CMO of Grand

Prix America who has also worked for the NFL's San Francisco 49ers and the NHL's New Jersey Devils: "I have two daughters, 10 and 13, and it absolutely kills me that they give trophies out for fifth and sixth place teams and participating. I think the reason sports is so valuable is it teaches you about sacrifice, how to deal with success and failure, individual and team accomplishments and goals, and how to work towards a common objective as a group that you may not even agree with some of the time but know it is for the better of the team."

NO MATTER WHAT YOU DO, SOMETIMES THINGS WILL FAIL

Can asking the right questions mitigate the chance of failure? Sure! Bennet James Bayer, former global CMO of Huawei Technologies, the largest telecommunications equipment maker in the world, sees this as a lost art, another problem with the way too many people learn and act today, and I'm inclined to agree with what he says: "If you don't want to buy my product or service, I need to find out why. Is it the product qualities? The color? The price? I don't see people practicing those skills as they used to. Part of the fun of the job for me is how I overcome problems and adversity. This is the difference between selling and telling. I think social media has led to more telling and more anti-social behavior. That is my biggest pet peeve. If you tell me you walked the cat today as part of a tweet to everyone, not only do I not care, I don't feel a personal connection. There is no personalization—no question back to me: Did you walk your cat today? Everyone talks; no one asks and then *listens*."

Yet even when you do listen and ask the right questions, that may not be enough. Michael Houlihan and Bonnie Harvey, co-founders of Barefoot Wine, America's number-one wine brand, launched its "California Beau" brand after the state dropped the legal limit of blood alcohol concentration for drunk driving to .08 percent from .1 percent. California Beau had half the alcohol of regular wine so women could drink the same one or two glasses and still stay below the legal limit. Great idea, right? "It failed miserably," said Michael. "People called the 800 number on the bottle and said, 'Now I have to drink twice as much to feel buzzed' or 'Why are you charging full price when it is only half the alcohol?' Californians loved the idea of keeping intoxicated people off the road but still wanted the buzz. They said they wanted to drink less alcohol, but they didn't. They were used to drinking two glasses. We just said, 'Done,' and ate the $100,000 we invested."

I like what Bonnie said to me about failure in light of that story: "I would like to eliminate the word failure from the English language. It really doesn't explain the process of learning." That works. Bonnie isn't pretending that California Beau succeeded, but she isn't celebrating its failure as evidence of her entrepreneurial spirit either. No one is going to die: I am going to succeed or learn.

Listen all you can. Look at the data. Ask the right questions. You still might fail. And that's OK. No one is going to die.

If people *were* going to die, I'd be dead or in jail facing many counts of murder. People constantly mock my choices and use any missteps as "proof of death." They flaunt my refusal to obey the numbers. They say, "My God, Jeff, what did you DO!?" and look at me with an expression somewhere between Edvard Munch's *The Scream* and Macaulay Culkin in *Home Alone*. All that has happened in my TV career alone. "They" laughed when I said, "This face belongs on TV," and then I made it on CNN, MSNBC, Fox Business Network, and shows like *Celebrity Apprentice*. They scoffed at my hubris when my first national TV pilot failed to get off the ground—and for even thinking it could. And when I reached my goal of having my own show on Bloomberg? They scoffed again when I pulled the show after one season and took it in-house as part of my own "C-Suite Network" (http://c-suitenetwork.com/) and the business channel on United Airlines (http://c-suitetv.com/).

Did I have any idea how to start a TV station when I launched the C-Suite Network and C-Suite TV? Of course I did! But I didn't know everything. Not even close. I didn't *need* to know everything. Momentum overcomes a lot of problems, and your passion fuels that momentum and drowns out the voices in your head that say "no" and tell you to act smaller.

Some leaders will say I'm crazy—not just the ones who think deeply on these kinds of tests but the people who say I am acting without data. "The data say it can't be done; the data say I'm going to lose one or more people in confronting the moral dilemma of the runaway train." Younger leaders are especially savvy about numbers. They've never *known* a time when loads of data weren't available. Data analytics, social media, and web-based marketing . . . so much is measurable today to help us make better decisions. But just because data are available doesn't mean you are getting the complete picture. Data don't tell you how and when to act, much like a recipe doesn't teach you how to cook, when to serve dinner, or whether your guests like bacon.

Of course I take the data into consideration, but my experience says that even if the data say "red" when I know it is "blue," it is blue. Even leaders at tech-based or data-driven companies, where they are completely drawn to the logic and clarity of numbers to help them make better business decisions, will tell you at the end of the day it is their ass on the line. They'd better believe the decisions in their gut and take responsibility for them—data or not.

That's what I do, and nobody, but *nobody* ever doubts my passion. *If you have that passion, you're ready to say, "Hey, watch this!"*

SOME OF THE BEST IDEAS START WITH SOMEONE SAYING "HEY, WATCH THIS!"

Some of the most terrifying experiences start that way, too—so do some of the worst ideas. We know "Hey, watch this!" is often code for "This is gonna be spectacular or this is gonna hurt—either way you'll get a show or a clip for *America's Funniest Home Videos*." Sometimes you don't know which one it will be until you experience it. But without passion, you'll never say "Hey, watch this!" with the conviction needed to deliver on your promise of something big.

Passion *can* override the voices saying no. It is the fuel for your climb to the top and the safety net for the bad landings.

Some of you who have read my previous books may be thinking, "Wait, Jeff, doesn't this contradict what you have said before? Didn't you say in *The Mirror Test* that you took a bath on pheasant farming all because your passion for a product got you so carried away?" Now why did you have to go and bring that up? Oh wait, I did . . . and the answer is, "No, it is not a contradiction." Passion *can* blind you from due diligence, but it will not take you in the wrong direction if you do the right things and keep listening as you go.

Passion *cannot* override the facts. Passion that pushes past facts becomes an indulgence. If the indulgence gets too big, you cross into obsession, and that's when you lose perspective.

> *Passion* can override the voices in your head saying no, but it can never override the facts.

The problem and the promise of passion is that it comes from your heart and your gut, not your head. Passion is defined as a strong and barely controllable emotion. That's why people feel like they constantly have to limit it; they don't like the lack of control that comes with it. Of course, passion leads us into bad decisions and doing some questionable things even when we have all the information we need. Remember that runaway train scenario? Most people interviewed on *Brain Games* said they would pull the lever to kill the one worker and save the bunch of people—unless their kid or someone else close to them was the worker. Then the reverse was true. I know that's honest. I know how I feel when someone wrongs my wife or hurts my kids. My passion for them can get me in trouble, because it is built on something genuine in my heart.

Maybe that's why I connect deepest to the passions of the people I meet, like Gene Simmons of KISS. He was my first interview for my CBS radio show, *All Business with Jeffrey Hayzlett* (www.play.it/allbusiness), but we had already met years before on *Celebrity Apprentice* when he was a contestant and I represented Kodak as one of the sponsors of a challenge. We butted heads a little about the results but stayed in touch and today have a great amount of mutual respect, even if we disagree on who is better looking. Gene is also exactly the same in person as he comes across onstage and on-screen. Last time I was at his home, he gave me a pair of thong underwear. Not a gift I expected from one corporate executive to another, but exactly what you'd expect from Gene Simmons. They chafe a little, but I digress . . .

While people know Gene Simmons the rock and reality television star, they don't see Gene Simmons the entrepreneur and marketing genius. Gene Simmons is a brand, and KISS is a big business that is now more than 40 years old and still at the top of its game, selling out concerts and merchandise. (KISS has licensed more than 3,000 products.) But Gene wasn't nearly as passionate about any of that as he was about telling me about starting his first business at 6 years old. He lived in a small village in Israel, and he and his friend went out and gathered cactus fruit, washed it, and sold it for a few pennies. He made two dollars that day, and after rewarding himself with an ice cream cone, he brought the rest of the money home and laid it on the table for his mother. At first, she was worried that he stole it, but when he told her the story, she said, "My little man."

That's the root of Gene Simmons' passion. Here is a guy, a millionaire in his sixties, and what drives him forward is the memory of what that ice cream tasted like and hearing his mother say those words when he was 6 years old. That's what fuels the fires he breathes literally onstage and figuratively in person. Peel back the face paint he wears, wipe off the blood he spits, and silence the ax-shaped bass he plays as part of his performance, and you find someone who does it all for his family.

Most of the biggest and best businesspeople I know tell some version of Gene's story as the root of what drives them. I know I do. We draw on that passion every day and never let it go as we push the proverbial envelope. We're not in it for the money. Well, we are and we aren't. We're in it for the money because that is how we keep score. That's how we build capital and get to do the things we have to, need to, and want to do for our businesses and families. But beyond that, we're in it for the adrenaline we get from pouring our passion into acting big in all we do in the most genuine way possible.

So if you fall flat on your face like my wife, Tami, did all those years ago, don't worry. Your family, friends, and the people who surround you in business will be there when you stand up. Don't let those face plants make you falter. Sometimes your passion and willingness to go "all in" might cost you, but no one is going to die. You're better off in the long run, when your passion will run up against other people's passions. You will need to be bigger to stand up to their attacks!

That's why I'm so passionate about everything I think my business can do. My partners or the market will remind me we don't have the time, resources, people, money, etc., to do all I dream about now. But if I start by limiting my passion, I can't do any of them. I also can't push my team forward. I might sound crazy at times, but that's the point: No one who says, "Hey, watch this!" with conviction is being completely rational.

LESSONS LEARNED: NO ONE IS GOING TO DIE

Repeat after me: No one is going to die. Say it: "No. One. Is. Going. To. Die." Nothing is ever going to be perfect. You're going to screw up. Things are going to not work. They might suck. You could even fail. *So what?* Stop celebrating failure as inevitable or a badge of honor for your entrepreneurial spirit. Succeed or learn and move on:

- No one is going to die when you think big and act bigger, so get over yourself.
- Stop overthinking things, coming up with reasons why not, and then playing it safe, and move! You still might fail. And that's okay. No one is going to die.
- Succeeding fast is better than failing fast: Stop wearing failure as a badge of honor.
- Passion fuels that momentum and drowns out the negative voices in your head.
- Passion can override the voices saying no, but it cannot override facts, lest it leads to overindulgence, obsession, and lost perspective.

Passion comes from our hearts and guts, not our heads. It's a strong emotion and can lead us into bad decisions and questionable actions. But it is the adrenaline we need to succeed. Without passion, you'll never know what it feels like to say, "Hey, watch this!" You'll never have the conviction needed to deliver on your promise to think and act big. Can that passion and willingness to go "all in" cost you? Perhaps. But no one is going to die. What's it going to cost you without it?

CHAPTER THREE

BE WILLING TO BE A LITTLE PIGHEADED AND IRRATIONAL

Push Harder and Farther Than You Have Before—No Excuses!

You may have noticed—and if you haven't, go ahead and say you did because you can—that I have told you to simultaneously embrace two opposite points of view in owning your story and developing your "no one is going to die" attitude:

"I want to do it, and you know what? I can do it, because I can."

and

"I don't want to do it, and you know what? I don't have to, because I can."

Successful leaders must constantly hold conflicting ideas, choices, possibilities, opportunities, and activities in their heads while thinking big and acting bigger in everything they do. I have never heard a better argument for why leaders must be relentlessly authentic in everything we do. In other words, go ahead and say, "Hell, yes!" *and* "Hell, no!"—just be consistently yourself no matter what you say! It is as important to strongly identify with what you don't want as with what you do. To truly find harmony in embracing the two sides of "because I can," you need to be not only nimble of mind, but also genuine in your character so people are willing to follow you even when you are a little *pigheaded* or *irrational.*

> *A sow doesn't care about turning its ear into a silk purse.*

PUSH HARDER: BE A LITTLE PIGHEADED

You know, I've been called pigheaded a number of times, and I've never taken offense, because I find pigs smart and delicious. But until this book, I never looked up the actual definition of pigheaded, which according to Merriam-Webster means "refusing to do what other people want or to change your opinion or the way you do something: very stubborn." Synonyms for pigheaded include everything from "headstrong" to "opinionated" to "willful." I'm good with being those things when necessary, especially when considering the opposites of pigheaded: "acquiescent, compliant, pliable, relenting, and yielding."

My only regrets in my business career are from when I wasn't pigheaded *enough.* I think back to Kodak and other situations where I went in thinking everyone was smarter than I was, so I dialed it back a bit instead of pushing harder. At Kodak, I should've fought tooth and nail to take the company private. I'm not sure other people were ready to do that or the other things needed to turn around the company, but honestly I also wasn't pigheaded enough to do the things I needed to do either. I have never let that happen again.

After that, I pushed—a lot. I pushed hard to have a business book bestseller as a first-time author. I pushed hard to land my national

TV show. I pushed hard to create my C-Suite Network, which I would now like to be the biggest business network in the world. What are the odds of that? Well, I already have one of the biggest egos . . . Okay, the odds are slim, but hey, someone is going to be number one, so why not me? Call me stupidly obstinate, but shooting for the possible is easy. Forget about being proud of picking the low-hanging fruit. I want to know what I have to do to make my company and me bigger, because it isn't *only* about me. It is about my family and the people who count on me in business and beyond. I want my team to check and balance me. I need my team to be a little pigheaded, not only to push themselves, but also to stand up to me when they think things are off. Otherwise I will keep moving in too many directions, spending my time trying to persuade them to do my bidding, or forcing my will on them with no checks and balances.

> *Push harder than you ever have to think big and act bigger—and not just in the greatest of circumstances, direst situations, and turning points.*

Wouldn't it be great to be part of a company with people saying, "We are, and we will!" while making things happen and having fun doing it? Of course it would. Are you willing to push people to do what it takes to think and act that way? That's why I am always trying to move people one way or another. Love me or hate me, just get off the fence and move.

When things start to move, I then expect my people to push back and push *me* harder. You want that tension and pushback. Make your people ask the really tough questions of what you are doing—and make sure you can answer them to find out where *you* are right and wrong— just like you do with them. After all, I'm not right *all* the time. I *believe* I am, but if my people can push and question me and help me find the answers, then we can do it bigger and better or pursue new directions that we align around as a team.

We can all do it or not do it together, because *we* can.

So why do leaders need to be so pigheaded? Why push so hard? The sad truth is sometimes people just want to do what they're doing and don't want to work as hard as they need to get the job done. I'm not going to get into the whole discussion of working hard vs. working smart, but I will repeat the line that the reason it's called work is that it's hard—really hard. I serve on a lot of boards and work with a lot of companies. Without fail, those that are really moving are doing the work that needs to be done together in the moment, 80 to 100 hours a week, barely sleeping. Because they *can*, they *want to*, and it is *fun*.

The companies that are going to die are empty at 5:30 P.M. That's how it was for me at Kodak. There was no one to join me at 2:00 A.M. so I wouldn't be the only person in a suit and tie eating the Garbage Plate at Nick Tahou Hots after a day of pushing hard to move the company forward. No push, no glory.

Yet being pigheaded is often not enough on its own to move a team.

PUSH FARTHER: BE A LITTLE IRRATIONAL

Peter Friedman, chairman and CEO of LiveWorld, a social media solutions company, started and ran Apple's first internet services division—creating and managing what today we call social networks. Apple used that community for marketing, customer support, and research market learning online, and it spawned companies like AOL and Salon. Of course, Apple embraced such forward thinking out of the gate, as it always sees the future before others, right? Wrong.

In 1994, when Peter presented his idea to the executive staff at Apple, he said, "'For now this will be used by some Mac and PC owners but eventually online communities will be much, much bigger than personal computers. They will be in phones, TVs, cars, and devices we haven't thought of yet. Everyone will use them in all aspects of their lives.' The room was quiet except for some grunting. I turned around to see they were covering their mouths because they were laughing at me. They're not laughing now."

Peter's story is a perfect illustration of why leaders constantly need to find ways to push things to the edge of (not off) the table. Even the most groundbreaking companies can get stuck and fail to see possibilities in the preposterous, because success is comfortable and often too connected to the past. As a result, it can be blinding. Peter pushed Apple to see future possibilities in an experimental project wrapped around community websites and kept pushing to create that internet services division in the nascent days of the web. Big thinkers know that's exactly when you must push harder and farther. We know the edge of the table is farther along than anyone else in the room. Like Peter, we keep pushing through the laughter behind our backs. Personally, I prefer people to laugh in my face. That way I can see everyone I need to wave

> *Nothing is ridiculous if you're willing to employ a little "irrational leadership."*

at as I pass them by doing what Peter did: employing a little "irrational leadership," swinging the pendulum way out there, stressing the system in such a way your people move faster and harder than they have before.

Greg Lucier, former CEO of Life Technologies, introduced me to the term "irrational leadership" at a talk I attended, and I remember thinking at the time, "What do you mean irrational? If anything, you want to be sane and rational in the C-Suite." Then I realized, of course you don't. As Greg noted, you have to be so far out there sometimes to pull people along to where you want them to go. You know they'll never be as irrational as you or as adamant about where you're going, so you put the goal way out there, even though people may see you as irrational. I had said for years that leaders need to create tension and results by pushing farther and farther to move the rest of their teams in that direction. Now I had a name for it.

Greg had to do this when he felt that Life Technologies, a group of aligned brands that researches cures for diseases like cancer and Alzheimer's by mapping the human genome, needed to push *away* from innovating at the cutting edge and look at the core value of what the company did, right down to changing the company name to Life Technologies and re-registering the company's symbol as LIFE. Changing a company name is always a radical move, but in this case it became a rallying cry and moved Life Technologies from being a house of brands to a branded house.

GET A LITTLE CRAZY—PUSH A ROPE!

To truly be irrational, you can't just push *hard;* you have to push *far*. You might even have to defy the laws of physics to do it. Take it from Brendan King, co-founder and CEO of Vendasta Technologies, a software company that builds essential marketing tools for digital agencies to sell to local businesses—he *has* a degree in physics: "In physics, we used to say, 'F = MA, and you can't push a rope.' In business, often you need to push a rope. You can pull all you want with the data, but sometimes you just need to push. An object at rest tends to stay at rest. Sometimes you have to push a rope, because people and things get stuck."

So how do you know where the edge of the table is when deploying a little "irrational leadership"? You don't, but for most of us the edge is much farther away than we think. If you are mostly comfortable, you aren't even close. If people at Apple are laughing behind your back, you're getting there. That's when you have to remember to tell yourself that you are not crazy. I'm not talking about "real crazy" like the people who warn me about "end of days" in emails or approach me with paranoid conspiracy theories at conferences. (To them, I just say, "I hear ya! Keep the faith, brother!" and keep walking.) I'm talking about "big thinking crazy." That's why every time someone says, "You're crazy" to me, I say, "Just wait, you'll catch up."

That's the way Kodak used to be. I remember talking to the "futurists" in the Kodak labs about a project that someone said couldn't be done because "physics doesn't allow it," and the futurists would say, "As we understand it now." As Kodak (where some of those future-minded engineers are still fighting to keep the company alive) and countless other companies have learned, it doesn't take long before crazy becomes the new normal in business. In fact, when you're a startup, small, or going through rapid change, crazy can seem like the norm. Heidi Lorenzen, former CMO of several Silicon Valley startups who also kept her sanity as a marketing executive at large tech companies, told me that is what she reminds herself every day: "Convincing myself that I am not insane is my biggest challenge. One day you are trying to be Picasso, the next day Einstein. One day I have my binoculars out, and the next day I am looking through a microscope. 'Just know you are not crazy, Heidi. Believe in yourself. If it is different, it does not mean that you are crazy, but that you are adding some value.'"

Exactly! It all goes back to being able to balance two conflicting or contradictory thoughts at all times—the irrational and rational, the push forward and the need to stay grounded. It is a dance. Not everyone will see your vision, but they need to know you can do more than pull the rope. You are pushing your teams and causing them stress in order for them to get agitated enough to be better customers inside the business—willing to buy into everything you could do and see themselves as essential to reaching what at first seems to be farfetched.

So take some time to cook a little crazy stew. Try this with your team:

- Ask them to come up with something audacious, unbelievable, beyond anything any of them have attempted before.
- Write all the ideas on the board.
- Let everyone rally around them.
- Be supportive, especially if they're pushing farther than they've gone.

How long did it take for the big thinking to start? Can they even do it? Do they start lapsing back into the rational and possible? If you told them to put the ideas into action, could they start? Or do they start complaining that it isn't real? Push them farther in reality to think big and act bigger. What happens when you do so can be transformative.

Think mutual funds for a moment, for example. Dave Pottruck, the former CEO of Charles Schwab, current chairman of Red Eagle Ventures, and author of *Stacking the Deck*, remembers a time in the early 1990s when the mutual funds industry was booming and Schwab's small equities business was going nowhere. So he asked his team the most challenging and seemingly irrational question: "What would we have to do in the next five years to become a player in mutual funds and reach a position where we can be competitive with Fidelity and Vanguard? How do we go from where we are today to be one of the Big Three players?"

The team realized that Charles Schwab's mutual funds service, which charged customers to buy or sell no-load funds, had to become free for them to use. That would attract more new and buying customers and make Schwab stand out from the crowd. That would also mean a complete shift in thinking at the company: putting the cost on the product manufacturers whose products they were distributing and servicing, not on the buyers, whom Schwab had been charging for more than eight years. This is usually where big thinking meets the wall separating it from big action, but Dave and his team pushed forward despite the seemingly irrational notion. The result was a huge win for Schwab, which moved into the Big Three in terms of mutual fund sales and was credited with transforming the distribution paradigm in the no-load mutual funds industry. That's the power of a question that pushes to the edge of the table. Had Dave asked a more modest question, like, "How do we increase growth from 10 percent to 15 percent?" he says, "We would have never had the guts to try for something so transformative and so bold. But the kind of growth we needed and were shooting for, over 100 percent per year, required a breakthrough idea." Ask the biggest question you can ask. You might be surprised at the "think big" answers it inspires in your team.

> *What are you doing to push beyond the usual outcomes and expectations? How will you hold people to higher standards than you ever had before? And how do you keep focus and balance—doing what you need to be doing—as you push to change?*

Start by asking a version of the question Dave did: *Now what?* You need to make sure that everyone who works for you is asking this question. The more people who are driven around the focus of where you want to go and push beyond perceived limitations, the more the company moves in that direction, the less irrational the CEO needs to be.

Think it sounds easy? Remember: "rational" is the central part of the word *rationalization*. Rational means "having logic or reason," and most of us can reason away anything; as Martin Luther once said, "Reason . . . is the Devil's greatest whore." Okay, Luther was talking about reason disconnected from faith, but the meaning applies here, too: Just as a whore serves those who pay, reason serves our need to explain and live with our failures. Those rationalizations are powerful excuses, and excuses are the gateway drug to thinking small and acting smaller. We *need* them. As Jeff Goldblum's character says in *The Big Chill*, "I don't know anyone who could get through the day without two or three juicy rationalizations. They're more important than sex. . . . Ever gone a week without a rationalization?"

OWN IT! NO EXCUSES!

When I first started in the speaking business, I did a recording of my talk "How to Rip the Head Off Your Competition." The title caught the attention of a national speakers' association, which listened to the recording, thought what I was doing was "positive and affirming," and asked me if I would offer to speak to some regional chapters. "Sure!" I said. I figured at worst it would be a nice way to get some traction, good for my other business, and great practice. So I wrote to the regional chapters and told them if they wanted me, I would come.

I immediately got a letter back from a woman at one group saying it was the "most arrogant presentation she had ever seen." She called it "derogatory" and "offensive," and then made it clear I was absolutely not what her group wanted. Um . . . then I read the letter again: "Seen?" She hadn't listened to my talk at all; she had just looked at the title, thought I was wrong, and rejected me.

I was disappointed, but I wasn't angry. In fact, I felt grateful, but I couldn't say why. Today, I can: The regional director rejected me because she could, but her reason was "because I can't." Perhaps she had owned her and her group's story by rejecting me, but it was a story with a thin premise—one that shut her down to possibility, opportunity, and learning. I was not "the way things are done," but based on what? Not a deep understanding of the material, just an excuse for saying, "I won't listen. We can't do this."

Like I said, I didn't understand all this at the time, but I did by the time something similar happened years later at TallGrass Public Relations. As I said before, the TallGrass name is the cornerstone of our motto: "To run with the big dogs, you've got to learn to pee in the tall grass." Yet in doing a revamp of our website, my team had taken down the motto. I was stunned and asked why. The answer?

"Because it offended some people."

When I think about my response, I know why I was grateful to that woman who rejected my presentation all those years ago: "Of course it offends people! That's my intent! If they are too offended to see past it, we don't want them. If we can't make them see past it, we aren't pushing them. And if we get rid of it, we aren't willing to stand up for it and be true to who we are. We need to step into it and own it."

> Excuses are the easiest answers to find, create the shortest stories to live in, and carry outsize weight in your fight against "because I can't."

We've been beaten to death with what we can't do, so we default to excuses for not doing things. Don't rock the boat! Don't offend people! But when you ask why people can't do something, you find they are just creating reasons to support the status quo or some limited worldview. They are looking for the next line in the small story they want to tell, not creating big stories that empower them to do more. This is why leaders need to be pigheaded and irrational sometimes.

A professor of mine at Augustana College in Sioux Falls, South Dakota, used to tell me stories about his Native American belief in "little people." These fairy-like creatures protected the tribe and warded off evil spirits and disease, but they were also prone to mischief and would whisper stories in your ear as you dreamed to make you say and do things you shouldn't. Little people carried outsize weight in Native American culture, and I like to think of them carrying outsize weight in ours, mischievously whispering excuses in our ears that turn us from action to inaction. Excuses like:

- It's not in the budget.
- We cut the budget.
- It's too expensive.
- It's too much work.
- New markets are tough.
- The market is too small to support that.
- The market wasn't ready.
- We can't see the ROI.
- The sales team said they can't sell it.
- We've always done it that way.
- We've never done that before.
- We tried it once before and it didn't work.
- That's not company policy.
- That's not the way we do it.
- It needs to be vetted by legal.
- You need to go through marketing.
- I needed to check with my supervisor.
- Facebook is more effective on Tuesdays.
- Everyone goes away during the summer.
- There's a [insert major weather event] there.
- You can't pitch on Fridays.
- No one responds to my emails.
- It's not newsworthy.
- Our audience is too old to understand that.
- Millennials act differently.
- We saw an article that said it was a waste of time, so we won't spend time on it.
- It's not my job to do that.
- No one told me what to do.

- That's not in my job description.
- That's not on my radar.
- That's not what I was told.
- I'm heading into a meeting.
- We're only open 8 to 6.
- I never saw the email.
- I didn't get the memo.
- I don't have the staff.
- It's a no-win scenario.
- It wasn't a fair fight.
- I thought someone else was handling this.
- I was waiting on something from someone else.
- I looked everywhere and couldn't find it.
- The file was too big to send.
- The internet was down and there's no wifi.
- My corrections were lost when the computer crashed.
- There was traffic/the train was late.
- My alarm did not go off.
- My phone is dead.
- I couldn't get a cab and Uber wasn't working.
- I just can't get anyone to agree on things.
- Our team just won't understand.
- We have to answer to our shareholders.
- We have to answer to our investors.
- I had a family emergency.
- My kid threw up (n.b.: applies to all child bodily fluids).
- I just work here.
- I don't have the bandwidth.
- I forgot.
- I just don't want to.
- They are going to beat me up in the parking lot for doing that.
- I saw a dog drowning in a ditch and had to save it.
- I had to give my cat dialysis.

I could go on and on, and I'm sure you could too. Tell me you didn't nod, smile, or roll your eyes when you read those excuses. We've all heard many of them before, and you're lying if you say you've never used one of them, even if it was in a harmless, innocent way. Maybe you dropped one to protect the feelings of someone you loved. Maybe you used one to cover up a larger problem you were trying to solve. Or maybe you used one because it was the *truth*. I am sure every one of these excuses has been true at some time. But remember: Excuses are easy, addictive, and designed to shut things down. Shit happened? Fine! What happened after you cleaned off your boots?

There's always a reason not to do something or an explanation why something did not happen in business, from the specific to the general to the ridiculous. Have you ever been in a meeting and heard someone say, "Hey, we can't do that because it's really expensive"? Of course it's expensive. It's also probably hard! *So now what?* I'll get deeper into ways to think differently later in the book, but for now ask yourself: What have you done to solve the problem, adjust your approach, or mitigate the damage? What do we need to do to get the job done? Don't stop!

I frequently meet people who say, "I'm in this situation and I know what I should be doing, but I can't get the people in front of me to do it." What that really amounts to is an excuse for not having a plan to push harder and farther. People who say that to me are *really* good at pointing out the problems but lousy at persuading people to fix them and thus can't push for solutions. Sometimes the solution is that you have to convince those people in front of you. That means you have to change their thinking.

I want my team to question things and push through their discomfort. I needed my team at TallGrass to question the naysayers about our motto and look at the hundreds of people who joined our Twitter profile because they loved our saying. I couldn't tell if my team was just using "other people" to mask their own discomfort with the motto, but that didn't matter. I have no patience for context when it comes to excuses. I need my people on the ground to write big stories without boundaries, not write a one-line short story that goes nowhere.

Like my team in the introduction, who were tasked with the plan for getting me a larger presence online but said they couldn't do it because of the budget, I want to push people to greater accountability, not abdication. When I ask you to go forth and get something done, I don't want to hear, "It's too expensive." I want to hear, "Jeff, it's going to require you to sell your ranch, but here's what it will accomplish . . ." They could have built a plan with costs, and I would have considered it. But that's not what they did. They came back with nothing based on presuppositions. God-dang it, just STOP. What's the worst that is going to happen? I don't approve? I may be a general, but this isn't war.

"No one is going to die" is easy to say, but harder to see, so push your people there. As long as everyone remembers what the mission is and stays focused even when you or they are being pigheaded or irrational, you'll filter out all the excuses and useless things that clutter our days. I can't tell you how many things I haven't needed to consider or have been able to rule out quickly simply because I focus as much as is humanly possible on who I am and what I'm in it for, which is where the next part of this story continues.

LESSONS LEARNED: BE A LITTLE PIGHEADED AND IRRATIONAL

Whether you're saying "I want to do it, and you know what? I can do it, because I can" or "I don't want to do it, and you know what? I don't have to, because I can," just be consistently, authentically you. This is never more necessary than when trying to get people to follow you when you are being a little pigheaded or irrational.

- → *Accept contradictory thoughts*: You need to be not only nimble of mind, but also genuine in your character to find harmony in embracing the opposites you will face every day.
- → *Push harder*: Be willing to be a little pigheaded in order to think big and act bigger.
- → *Push farther*: Be a little irrational and push the rope! Nothing is ridiculous if you're willing to employ a little "irrational leadership," stressing the system in such a way that people move faster and harder than they have before.

➤ *Push past the rational*: Excuses are the easiest answers to find, create the shortest stories to live in, and carry outsize weight in your fight against "because I can't."

Leaders need to push hard, because success is comfortable and people often want to keep doing what they're doing and not work as hard as they need to to get the job done. Success can also trap you in the past. To change their thinking, we must make our people question things and have zero tolerance for excuses. We need them to write big stories without boundaries, not one-line short stories based on presuppositions and assumptions that go nowhere.

PART TWO

FOCUS IT!

CHAPTER FOUR

KILL THE SQUIRREL

Focus on What Matters

My favorite scene in the Pixar movie *Up* is when the old man Carl and the boy Russell get stranded near Paradise Falls and meet Dug the talking dog. When Russell asks Dug to speak, he actually *does*: "Hi there! My name is Dug. I have just met you and I love you!" Dug jumps on Carl and excitedly continues explaining as the two humans stare, shocked and incredulous, "My Master made me this collar. He is a good and smart Master, and he made me this collar so that I may talk. . . ."

Dug suddenly stops, shoots his head distractedly to the left, and shouts: "SQUIRREL!"

> I know when to "kill the squirrel," and so must you.

Anyone who owns or has even seen a dog understands the joke, which becomes a running bit throughout the movie. Even in the most important and dire situations, "squirrels" distract Dug and the other talking dogs. I'm certainly guilty of Dug-like behavior on a regular basis, but I am also maniacal about focusing when it matters.

If you are a business leader trying to think big and act bigger, you must be the Big Dog and "up," but you can't be Dug in *Up*. You can do and own everything we have covered so far, but if you do not relentlessly focus that ownership on what drives your business, create a culture that reflects who you are, and stay grounded as you make things happen, you will never see the true rewards of thinking big and acting bigger. You will be all over the place.

Sure, we all like to do different things and get caught up in this project or that idea, but we must ensure we—*and* our teams—can answer these questions easily and directly:

- ➤ Beyond our conditions of satisfaction, what's the one thing driving our business, and what are we doing to drive it further?
- ➤ Is doing that thing going to lead to things you *really* want and need to get done?
- ➤ What is the behavior we want to drive?
- ➤ Why are we doing what we're doing?

That last question is one people do not take the time to ask out loud. Try it, and see what kind of answers you or your team give. More likely than not, you'll be surprised at what they *and* you say. Asking big questions is easier than thinking about and acting on them. *But you must, because as this cowboy knows, you can't go in if you don't know the way out.*

FOCUS ON THE RIGHT SQUIRRELS

My family is perhaps never more annoyed with me than when they ask me where I want to go to dinner and I immediately answer, "[Here]."

Come to think of it, my office families express the same annoyance about the choices I make for my businesses. The conversation then goes something like this:

"You answered too quickly!" they tell me.

"Would you like me to say it slower?" I reply.

"But you didn't consider the other possibilities," they say.

"Sure I did. I considered the possibilities, and I don't like them."

"You didn't give anything else a chance," they say.

"Yes, I did. My chances just come a lot faster. Wait, wait . . . let me think again [pause, look up]. . . . No! Does that make you feel better?"

Am I being a little pigheaded? Perhaps, but that's not the point. My point is I have filtered the noise to focus quickly and efficiently on what needs to be addressed. I do not want to waste time thinking about the thousands of choices I could make when the choice I make is good enough. These decisions are not what matters to thinking big and acting bigger. Since I have a constant awareness of and real clarity about what drives my business and me, I am able to focus quickly on easy answers, which is good because focus can be a real problem for people like me, who look at a blank wall and see opportunity. The reactor rods of my brain are being raised out of the water all the time, and with caffeine, that happens at an accelerated rate of at least ten.

That's why when a friend asked me if I could go back in time for ten seconds to offer one piece of advice to myself at any point in my career, I couldn't think of specifically where I would go, but I knew exactly what I would say to a younger me: "Kill the squirrels and focus."

It's not just the imaginary squirrels I need to kill. Sometimes there are real squirrels to chase, and I know if I catch them they could be deliciously profitable. So first I need to separate the fake squirrels from the real ones and then decide which ones are worth chasing. The problem is that I always think I see squirrels even in the biggest piles of manure. I knew that my Dug-like pursuits had to end the day I looked at my to-do list and found 389 things on there. Talk about a pile of "Holy crap, are you kidding?" Granted, some of the list was minutiae, but if my to-do list exceeds the number of days in the year,

> *Focus not just on what needs to be done but on how much time you will spend on it.*

how can I claim any focus at all? *I had to learn to filter out what did not matter so my energy could focus on what did.*

The only thing no one in the history of the world has learned to make more of is time. Without managing your time, anything you do, no matter the size or importance, can cause you to fall victim to Parkinson's Law: Work expands to take up the time available to finish it. I had to learn to filter my projects through the time I had, not the time I dreamed I had, to get through the day, week, month, and year.

My solution was to get in shape—a triangle, that is. I drew an inverted triangle (with the base at the top of the page). I then divided it into even thirds horizontally, so the biggest space was at the top. Finally, I filled in my list of tasks as follows:

- In the top, or biggest third, are the things I need to spend most of my time on.
- In the middle are things I spend some of my time on.
- In the bottom are the things I should spend the least of my time on.

The key to the triangle, however, is not simply dividing tasks into time: *It is leaving tasks off the triangle completely.* As I said, I see everything as critical, important, or a moneymaking opportunity, but just as if everybody wins then no one wins, if everything is important, then *nothing* is. Everything is thus directionless. Now I may be spending less time on some things, but they were still important enough to make the triangle, and I can plot my way through them. The other squirrels have been squashed (at least for now). (See Figure 4–1 on page 53 and Figure 4–2 on page 54.)

Pushing some things off or crossing them off completely no matter how passionate I was about them is always the hardest part of this exercise. I still fail at it occasionally. For example, a year after launching the C-Suite Network and exploring how to expand it in every possible way, my partner confronted me and told me I had

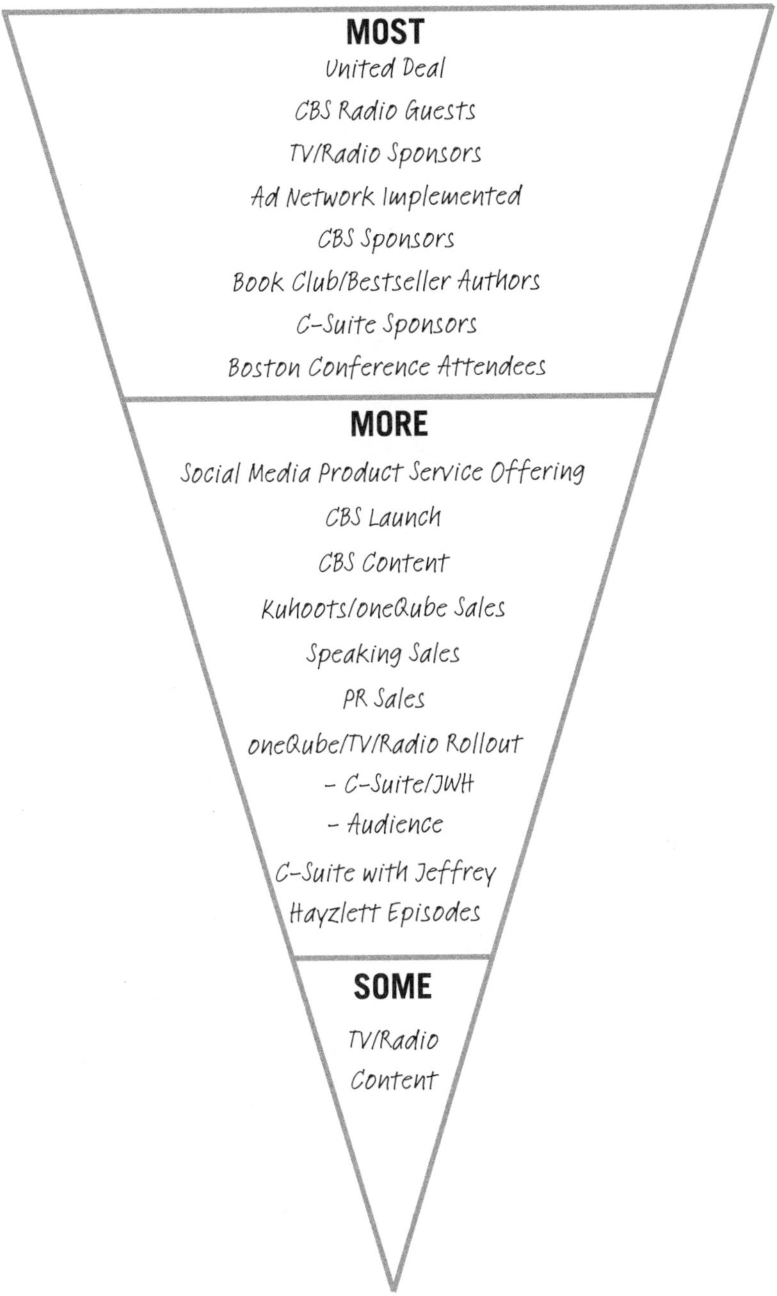

MOST

United Deal

CBS Radio Guests

TV/Radio Sponsors

Ad Network Implemented

CBS Sponsors

Book Club/Bestseller Authors

C-Suite Sponsors

Boston Conference Attendees

MORE

Social Media Product Service Offering

CBS Launch

CBS Content

Kuhoots/oneQube Sales

Speaking Sales

PR Sales

oneQube/TV/Radio Rollout

– C-Suite/JWH

– Audience

C-Suite with Jeffrey

Hayzlett Episodes

SOME

TV/Radio

Content

Figure 4-1—A "focus" triangle of mine from January 2015

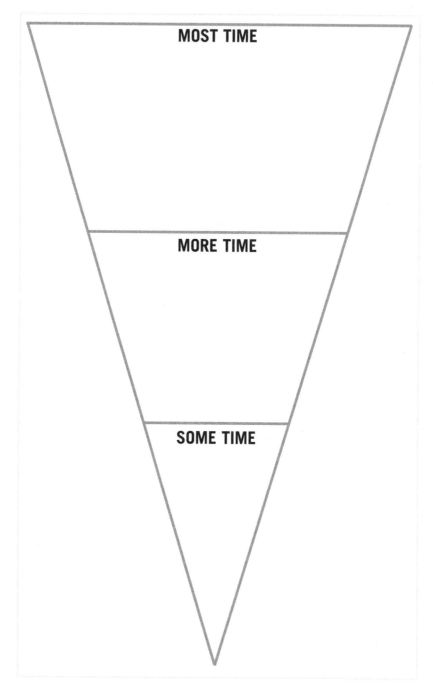

Figure 4-2—Sample focus triangle

started too many things. He was right. Sure, I needed to do some of it to test where we could go, and it all will absolutely be helpful in the future and probably lead to a greater valuation down the road. But . . .

Will it cause us some problems over the short term? Yes.

Could it have cost us everything? Yes.

Do we need those hassles? NO.

Therein lie the issues—and the dance—between opportunity and distraction. Understanding the limits on my time forces me to address the important questions and focuses my ongoing pursuit and completion of the biggest, most important things.

This focus not only helps me complete the things in my triangle, but also makes me say "no" much earlier than I ever have, both to the things I shouldn't do and the things I desperately want to say yes to and know I could kick ass on but just can't right now. The fun new things? The sexiest things? The coolest things? They may look tempting (and fun, cool, and sexy), but where will they lead me? If I am already busier than a one-legged man in a butt-kicking contest, can I really kick any more ass? This is why I take vacations—to do those things not on my triangle, so I'm not consumed with that desire daily.

Now, you might ask: Is all this a moving target? Of course it is—this is part of the dance, too! I constantly need to change the focus of what things are in my triangle, and I need additional triangles to focus on different parts of my business. My "triangle scheme" may not be right for you; the important thing is that you find a similar (and equally adaptable) way to plan your time and resources.

Of course, whatever tool you choose, you'll still chase some rogue squirrels—and a few that were never there. It's in our nature to do so. We're always going to find ourselves saying "Hey, watch this!" now and again. I still do ten things at once. How can I not? That's part of the dance, too. If I need to step out of a dinner and take a call from India in the restaurant storeroom, I will. What I'm talking about is spending time on the ten *most important* things at once, especially when it comes to our clients and customers.

FOCUS ON THE RIGHT BUSINESS

I interviewed Peter Philippi, CEO of Strategex, for one of my C-Suite Network Conferences (http://c-suitetv.com/video/executive-perspectives-peter-philippi/). The conferences focus on the professional development of networking leaders in businesses from $10 million to $100 million in revenue. Strategex creates customized growth strategies for mid-to-large B2B organizations, and Peter has an interesting take on the Pareto Principle, or the 80/20 Rule, which many leaders often use for evaluating people, customers, and more results-driven tasks. I have used it in broad strokes to deal with tasks, time, talent, and most of all *me*, because you cannot expect your business to follow a rule without owning it yourself.

Here's a little background for those of you who don't use the principle or who might know it in name but have no idea what it is or its origin. The Pareto Principle dates back to 1906 and an Italian economist named Vilfredo Pareto. Pareto studied the patterns of money and wealth in Switzerland and discovered that 80 percent of the nation's land was controlled by just 20 percent of the population. He also found the same pattern in other countries. Other economists took a cue from Pareto and started noticing similar unequal patterns in which a small amount of "causes" accounted for a disproportionate number of "effects." This disparity between cause and effect is what became known as the Pareto Principle, or the 80/20 Rule. Most often, it is a general rule in business that the top 20 percent of your customers account for 80 percent of your revenue.

As I said earlier, rules are meant to be broken, and even Pareto can be used as an excuse for ignoring potential or self-fulfilling prophecy. ("I was only focusing on the top 20 percent because that's what Pareto told me to do.") But Peter's take on it is about anything but excuses. I wanted our C-Suite Network to hear him run through his company's signature tool (his version of the 80/20 Rule), because its focus is on *focus*. Here's what he has you do:

> ➤ Make a list of all your customers from a 12-month period.
> ➤ Organize the list in descending order of revenue.

> ➤ Split the list into four equal groups, with the top being the top 25 percent in terms of revenue and the bottom the bottom 25 percent.

According to Peter, "You will see that the top 25 percent accounts for 89 percent of your revenue, the second 25 percent accounts for 7 percent, 3 percent on the third, and 1 percent on the bottom. Directionally that is always the case in business-to-business, like manufacturing, distribution, and some service organizations." Peter is so sure of this formula that he has those numbers printed on the back of his business card: 89, 7, 3, and 1.

It seems to me, then, that by focusing on growing the top 25 percent—the "whales," as Peter calls them—and maybe some of the highest-growth customers in the next three groups, and spending less time on the rest (what Peter calls "minnows"), a business could make a lot more money. But as Peter told me, most businesses don't do that— even the ones who buy into everything he says. At least not right away. He has seen this time and time again after he presents. *Why?* Focus, focus, focus. When people say, "I don't see the bigger thing to act on," what they often mean is they won't focus on the big questions and answers, can't focus on them, or don't want to see them at all.

Why won't you focus? Why can't you focus? Why don't you want to focus?

Won't Focus

Some people just won't do the hard work they need to do. I have nothing more to say to you people.

Can't Focus

The truth is, adjusting to big thinking and bigger action from everything in this book to more targeted acts like Peter's takes time. "All in" is great, but I'm fine with the value slowly sinking in—at least it eventually does. More often, people like myself, Peter, and other speakers and consultants are battling against "Monday Morning Effect," in which people come back to the office after going to a speech, event, or conference (often over a weekend, hence the name) and are immediately inundated with day-to-day business. They soon forget completely about all the things they learned and wanted to implement. As compelling as I am, once I am off the stage or you turn the page, my words are memories competing for your attention. That's why time comes into focus in this chapter. The more someone focuses time on what matters, the greater the chance they will act.

Sometimes, however, "can't focus" has less to do with time and distractions than resources and tools: You lack the resources, tools, and information to answer the questions you have. My question here is: Are you sure that tool or information cannot be had, or are you making another excuse for not focusing and acting? Are you sure the answers aren't there? And if they aren't, can you do something about that to create more opportunity? Innovation can be anywhere in business.

Solving a "can't focus" problem is why Jeff Winsper built his latest venture, Black Ink, in 2013: He needed answers that would help him and other contemporary marketers focus where they couldn't before. Black Ink offers a sales and marketing analytics software platform to help C-Suite people and day-to-day revenue generators get a better handle on key performance indicators. What's so special about that? Up until then, there had been zero top-down business-level reporting to validate marketing performance using empirical evidence that met financial reporting requirements. *Zero.* You can't measure what doesn't exist—even for the companies with the biggest resources and most innovative programs!

Jeff had spent 15 years looking for a solution—using data, modeling, advanced analytics, Generally Accepted Accounting Principles, reporting standards, and other methods. But until recently, the right set of data was hard to access and evaluate, and nearly impossible to model with accuracy. Still, Jeff resolved to push forward, recalling the words of the CFO of a large consumer packaged goods company, who told him anyone who asked for a sales and marketing budget had to answer two very simple questions: What was the value of your last dollar spent?

And what will be the value of your next dollar spent? "In marketing, answering those simple questions has been vexing and problematic for years," says Jeff. "Marketing is a social science, not a physical science; there is no exact right and wrong—only continuous learning and improving. This is not to be confused with the desire to understand the 'Science of Marketing.' Quite simply, it is pretty perplexing to know where to spend budgets moving forward if you don't have at least some understanding of marketing's ROI performance today. For years, marketing leaders were using qualitative, squishy language to answer the CFO's questions. Remember, boardroom language is quantitative, and anything less is met with skepticism.

"Today, businesses can now use advanced sales and marketing analytics that demystifies marketing and puts it in plain speak to arm everyone with evidence," Jeff continues. Black Ink allows marketers to celebrate their success quantitatively—to proudly stand up and say, "I generate revenue for my company. Fifteen years later, we can quantitatively measure marketing value. Now, if a CFO says, 'Where should I spend my money this quarter?', we can tell them. 'Who should I go after and why?' Bam, we have that answer too. For example, we have a customer that has been in business for 20 years, generating billions annually, and is growing profitably. With Black Ink, we identified $200 million of incremental revenue opportunity by focusing on what can be done, which couldn't have been realized before."

Don't Want to Focus

This is the stickiest of the focusing problems, and for many leaders, especially those in the C-Suite, there are consequences that go beyond business. I invited David Meinz, director of the Executive Heart Program, which offers an advanced approach to preventing heart attacks and strokes in business leaders, to speak to my C-Suite Network in order drive this point home. "The biggest killer of C-Suite executives is cardiovascular disease. The most common first symptom of cardiovascular disease is sudden death. Again, death is the most common *first* symptom," says David. "The biggest mistake most executives make is in believing that everything's OK if they eat well, exercise, and their cholesterol numbers are good. It's important to realize that science has now gone way beyond cholesterol levels and that most physicians, well-meaning as they are, are about ten years behind in prevention of heart disease and stroke. Yes, *your* physician, too. Even though we all have auto insurance, we still invest time and money to maintain our cars with oil changes and tune-ups. But when it comes to our heart, most executives pretty much just assume everything is fine. In half of the cases, if they have a heart attack or stroke, they don't ever get a second chance. Most C-level executives are not focused enough on fighting the biggest threat to their health and life. If you die prematurely from a heart attack, what will that mean to your family? Even if you survive a stroke, how good of a leader are you going to be?"

When it comes down to what David says, someone is going to die, and that's why I finally focused my bacon-loving butt on my heart, got treated, lost 40 pounds, and started to exercise more—and so should you. When it comes down to what Peter says, no one is going to die, but focusing is just as hard because it is often deeply personal: "One of the big issues in getting leaders to make these decisions is the emotional attachment to certain customers, products, services, and employees. They don't want to make the hard decisions to make their business better. In this case, they're making a lot more money in the top and losing money in the bottom. When we bring that to light then they are ready to make decisions—if they are willing to do it unemotionally."

I have written many times about acting unemotionally when it comes to firing people and customers, but one point bears repeating here: The problem is we are trained to treat everyone the same, but they are not the same. Some customers, products, services, and employees *are* better than others. You've got to find a way to deal with the underperformers, and if that means "we love you, we'll miss you, but you're fired," that's okay. Just deal with them thoughtfully but directly so you can be done with them and deal more with the bigger picture.

When it comes to customers this is hard, especially for entrepreneurs who grew their businesses with a few loyal early-adopting customers and now find those customers are minnows in the bottom quarter of a list like Peter's. The connection is deep, but the revenue is shallow.

From servicing them through secondary channels to finding their business another home that will give them the attention they deserve, you must find a way to help them, and then you must let them go.

FOCUS ON THE RIGHT "MATTER"

As I thought about what Peter said, I also began thinking about Millennials—who will soon make up the majority of the American work force—and whether things might be different for them. A lot of stories talk about Millennials being different from past generations—that they are buying, doing, and participating based on their values, while previous generations tended to care about values *after* they have made money. The media and our popular culture are filled with items about how Millennials want purpose-driven companies and missions beyond or in place of the bottom line. They love their "minnows."

I have heard more than a few businesspeople of my generation look down on these Millennials for these and other reasons, calling them entitled, lazy, and crazy. Millennials, "they" say, don't want to focus with a real "because I can" attitude of the "I don't want to do it, and you know what? I don't have to, because I can" variety. I am sure there is truth on both sides of the story, but I pass no judgment. No, that's incorrect. I do pass the same judgment on everyone, whether they are young or old, purpose-driven or profit-driven: *Who you are and when you were born is irrelevant; no one can survive without focusing in their own way on what matters and drives their business.*

As I write this book, my business focus is on speaking, because I love it and strive to make every keynote I give special, but also because every time I speak, I get paid, marketed by the group or company that hired me, booked for more gigs, generate business for my public relations firm, asked to join a board of directors, and make lots of new connections. Speaking is so powerful I would even take the stage for the right group for free if it will lead to those other things on the list. If a group can put me in front of leaders at high-growth companies or thousands of people who manage businesses, associations, and franchises who could book me into *their* companies, I am available now.

That said, I tell the team to get these speaking gigs for me. I don't see most of the process anymore, nor should I. I don't have the time. *Once I've done it and know how to teach it, I don't need to be involved in the process. I can have my team do it for me. My focus is needed somewhere else.*

FOCUS THE TEAM ON THE RIGHT THINGS

My team has the power to solicit on my behalf, have meetings with potential clients, and say yes or no just as fast as I make a decision on dinner, because we have a system that empowers them to make those decisions. *No one* should be offended by this approach (i.e., they do not get to speak to me directly). It is designed to speed the start of a relationship by focusing on what matters or stop conversations before they get started so neither side wastes any time.

Make sure your team remembers what matters, where things are going, and what you want to build.

Every entrepreneur goes through this same evolution and can't wait to get to this point in their business: We start as one-man bands; then we add devout followers; and then we move beyond that to make it a real business, adding skilled technicians and professionals who give us the scale we need to grow from one to many zeroes. We can go through these steps slowly or rapidly, but how successfully we do it is directly proportional to how much our people understand what matters and where you and the business are going so they can align around you and check you as you grow. That's an essential step in focus *and* empowerment.

Getting your team to do this is as simple as asking questions like, "What can we do better next time?" When I leave a meeting, when we are blocks away or in a car on the way home—even when we kicked ass—I always ask, "What could we have done better? How can we improve?" In fact, answering these questions is even more fun when we kicked ass, because it feels good to focus on just how much better it could be. That's why the Katelyn Rule from Chapter 1 is also important here: Leaders need to stop employees from asking unnecessary questions, which empowers those employees to ask and answer the right ones on their own.

But there is an even more treacherous character to present in the last part of this story, and it brings us back to where we began this chapter. These insidious characters, however, are not squirrels who distract me like they did Dug the talking dog in *Up*; they are the ones who think *I'm* Dug, and like the Alpha dog in the movie, they think they have "strength and cunning" I do not.

Let me introduce Mr. TYCO.

Sometimes I hire people who are smarter than I am; that's why I hire them. But sometimes those people think that makes me stupid. In one case, I hired a gentleman I felt could really help expand our marketing. Instead, he constantly tried to teach *me* marketing.

I don't mean to pat myself on the back, but most people I meet and (almost) all the people I hire know that marketing is something I have a fairly solid grasp of and have constantly innovated in. I have even won my share of awards. But this person felt an insatiable need to make sure I understood what I was talking about and explain to me how certain things should be done—while we were already doing things that way.

Now, I liked this guy. I felt he added value in his breadth of experience and youthful energy. So at first I pointed out that he really didn't need to be doing that. "I understand," I said, directly but nicely. "I do understand why people respond certain ways. I do understand what SEO is and how ad networks work. I usually go out of my way to get educated on things we do, because I have to know what it is and how it works before I start making decisions about it."

That seemed to work . . . for a day or so. Then it started again. It became such an issue that 30 percent of every conversation was being eaten up by this guy saying, "Let me explain to you how this works" and me saying, "I don't need you to explain this."

Finally I just started replying "TYCO." He would explain something in person or in an email, and I would reply, "TYCO." After about the third or fourth time, he finally asked, "So what does this TYCO mean?"

And I replied, "Thank you, Captain Obvious."

"I didn't hire you to teach me the things I already know," I continued. "I hired you to do the things I don't know or teach me things I don't know, not to take me to areas I can get to by myself. Otherwise, why do I need you?"

TYCO is the G-rated version of NSS (No Shit, Sherlock). TYCOs get me bogged down in process I don't need to focus on anymore. Or, as I like to say, "Focus and just give me the cake, TYCO." I *love* cake, and I appreciate that you made it. But I don't have time to hear about the process of making the cake. I don't need to know about the frosting and how long it took to bake, and I sure as heck don't want to talk about baking the cake *while it is baking*. I want my people to understand I've baked a lot of cakes in my lifetime, so I don't need to learn how anymore; what they need to focus on is bringing me the right and most delicious cake. I just want to focus on eating it so I don't get hungry while I cook up the future of the business.

Knowledge is critical in a business. Implementation of that knowledge is even more critical. In football terms, I like quarterbacks who complete passes, running backs who can gain yards, receivers who can catch passes, linemen who can block or sack quarterbacks, and kickers who can put the ball through the uprights. I don't sign up players unless they already know they need to do those things, so I don't need them to tell me that's what they do. I don't need a kicker to tell me, "The only time I score is when I put it through the uprights."

TYCO.

Too many people want to spend their time telling you what they know and then showing you how to win. The winners just do it.

LESSONS LEARNED: KILL THE SQUIRREL

You must relentlessly focus on what drives your business, or you will never see the true rewards of thinking big and acting bigger. You can own your story, believe no one is going to die, and push as hard as you can while being a little pigheaded and irrational, but it will mean nothing if you fail to filter the noise, learn the dance between opportunity and distraction, and focus on what matters.

- Beyond you and your conditions of satisfaction, what's the one thing driving your business, and what are you doing to drive it farther? Constantly ask and answer the essential questions about your business to test and develop your focus.
- You can't manufacture time, so make more of it by filtering out what does not matter so your energy is focused on what does.
- Stop making excuses for why you won't, can't, or don't want to focus on the big questions and answers.
- Focus *and* empower your team by ensuring they remember what matters, where things are going, and what you want to build—especially the TYCOs.

That last step is crucial. Our people—the devout followers, skilled technicians, and professionals—give us the ability to scale and grow from one to many zeroes in revenue. How successfully we do it is directly proportional to how much your people understand what matters and where you and the business are going, so they can align around you and check you as you grow.

CHAPTER FIVE

DEVELOP YOUR OWN FLOW

Cadence Matters!

A few years ago, I was with a group of friends in the tribal offices of an Native American reservation, waiting to get our hunting permits for that day. The woman at the desk asked for our driver's licenses, and my friend and I stepped forward first. My friend is a foot shorter than me, bald, and has a moustache, which at the time I did not. But still the woman at the desk kept getting our information and pictures confused.

Finally, she turned to us and said, "All you white people look the same to me."

No matter how much you *think* you are different, you are not. If you can take the nature and name of your company out of your strategic plan, drop someone else's in, and it works the same, what's your difference? Do you think that your messaging, idea, packaging, service, food, marketing, interface, design, etc., are so much better, perhaps even unique, because you look different? No, we are all the same. And if for some lucky reason you are actually unique now? Just wait.

It does not matter how different our industries are or what we sell, how large or small our companies are, or how long we've been in business. Every business has just three points of difference when it comes to its look and feel and thinking big and acting bigger: you, your people, and your cadence. Of these three, cadence, and the systems and culture that stem from it, gets the shortest shrift but has a deep and disproportionate effect on your people's morale—more than you alone

Your look and feel must be exactly that— yours.

ever could. How many people leave a company of some scale because they don't like the CEO? Most people who leave a company they don't like working at do so because of a poisonous cadence: ineffective systems, a culture that makes them feel undervalued, and bad relationships with the people they work with and answer to. That ultimately stems from you and the cadence you create. That's why focusing on cadence is essential. If your business's cadence is not genuinely and completely reflective of what matters to you, your people will never forge a connection to it and have the loyalty you need.

WHAT'S YOUR CADENCE?

Ever notice in movies or on TV shows that when there are scenes in businesses—whether they are comedies or dramas—the offices are basically characters? The staid grey formal C-suite of the big law firm or multinational conglomerate suggests the soulless seat of the powerful in their suits and ties. The brightly colored, couch- and foosball table–filled open space of the tech startup indicates the free spirit of the Millennials in hipster jeans and flannel.

How an office looks, what the rules are, who sits where, who speaks and why, what goes right and what goes wrong with its systems may sound superficial for thinking big and acting bigger, but that's far from the truth. Whatever and wherever the office is and where and how its big decisions are made reflects the culture of the organization—its personality and emotional connection to anyone it touches. That is key to its cadence.

Cadence is your company's river—its culture and systems—and the more it flows in a way that works for your company, the more it flows through anyone it touches, from employees to vendors to customers. You must develop and focus this flow as it supports and guides you through the process of thinking big and acting bigger. It is the energy of your business, and just like energy, you can draw on different and alternative resources to power your business. But you must draw on your own power source. Inspiration is fine, but don't bother looking through someone else's eyes in addressing your cadence.

What your company looks like and how it acts reflects the culture of your organization, and the systems of the culture reflect who you are.

A business must pay close attention to align its teams around its cadence, because that's how they pick up the flow to think and act bigger. Cadences can be very different, but they must be disciplined, whether extremely formal and expansive or informal and intimate or anywhere in between. Just know that whatever your cadence is, it "broadcasts" your culture from the boardroom to the front door and across all your platforms to anyone it reaches.

I always knew this was the case, but I never realized how different cadence could be until I walked into the offices of CrossFit to shoot an episode of the *C-Suite with Jeffrey Hayzlett* (http://c-suitetv.com/video/crossfit-craze-c-suite-with-jeffrey-hayzlett/). When I was with Kodak, everything was very traditional, right up to the big round fine mahogany table in the C-suite that could seat 15 people in big leather chairs. Executive meetings in that room looked like the Knights of the Round Table. But that's where Kodak came from: It had a formal history, and its corporate culture reflected that. It was one of the reasons I struggled as a change agent there: Kodak had been stuck in those traditions for decades and struggled to compete against companies that had a different cadence—cultures of change that were nimble enough to respond to the rapid pace of business.

I haven't had that kind of formality when it comes to my businesses, but I still have a fairly traditional cadence. Contrast my experiences with CrossFit, a fitness company with more than 11,000 affiliates nationwide that is part of a wave of workout studios transforming the fitness industry with different, bigger thinking. CrossFit caters to workout junkies. It doesn't matter if they are Navy SEALs or supermoms, only that they embrace and dedicate themselves to the CrossFit difference. CrossFit supports their lifestyles by building their programs, communities, and affiliates around them (http://c-suitetv.com/video/crossfit-craze-c-suite-with-jeffrey-hayzlett/). Those affiliates can be a few hundred square feet supporting a small membership or as big as any fitness center you have ever seen.

None of that would be possible, let alone sustainable, if CrossFit's cadence as a company did not match what was happening at those affiliates. That is key to their success. The day I interviewed founder and CEO Greg Glassman at the company's Santa Cruz, California, headquarters, he came in wearing a T-shirt with a Pablo Picasso drawing of a naked woman. That said everything about his personality, reflected his status as a rebel within the fitness industry, and captured the cadence of the company. CrossFit's flow was like the Picasso on Greg's shirt: modern and revolutionary for its time. His team told me that they have meetings at barbecues or on a jog, and while more formal meetings in the office do happen, they have no printed agendas, briefing books, or binders. Instead, everyone has a laptop or a tablet and is always prepared to keep things moving and find any information needed on the spot.

I was blown away—not only because it was so different, but also because it reaffirmed, in a way I had never seen before, the rewards of a company's cadence to thinking and acting bigger. What looked like disorder to my more formal corporate eye was very well-defined and deliberate, just like CrossFit's business. It was efficient despite constant movement and like its affiliates: organic, informal, intimate, and a workout that works.

CrossFit may not be traditional in its thinking or cadence, but a company does not have to be contrarian to have a genuine cadence that reflects the brand. Consider Dunkin' Donuts. It's a $9 billion company that felt familiar to me in its corporate look and feel. But what sets it apart from other franchisers is its cadence. Dunkin' Donuts realized early on that they weren't in the business of selling franchises; they were in the business of growing their franchisees' businesses, which generated the majority of the brand's income. So they developed a cadence that operated like the stores—everyone in at headquarters when it's "time to make the donuts."

This proved to be true when I arrived at 6:30 A.M. at Dunkin' Donuts headquarters in Canton, Massachusetts (http://c-suitetv.com/video/dunkin-brands-c-suite-with-jeffrey-hayzlett/). The lobby was full and the executives were all there; they come in early just like the bakers and franchisees and long before the morning rush. By 5:30 A.M., they're looking at numbers from the day before and weather reports from across the country, seeing what impact they might have on their franchisees' businesses, and discussing what they might do to help. It was refreshing and filled the company with a healthy buzz (although some of that may have been caffeine induced from Dunkin' Donuts famous coffee). It was a cadence that reflected the look and feel of the brand.

Like any company, Dunkin' Donuts and CrossFit will need to make sure their cadences stay reflective of who they are as they grow, refresh, and extend their brands (domestically at the moment for CrossFit, internationally for Dunkin' Donuts). Their cadences will help everyone who works for and with them remember who they are, because that's the only way any company can ensure its greatest point of difference—its people—are aligned, buy in 100 percent, and push themselves to think and act bigger as the company pushes forward.

Of course, a business does not have to be as big as Dunkin' Donuts or CrossFit to be this way. Any size business, from one to 1 million employees or more, that has a genuine cadence not only defines its identity, but also commands a deeper loyalty.

Ask yourself: Does your business have a cadence that reflects who you are? If the answer is no, why not? But before you answer, I refer you back to the list of excuses in Chapter 3. "I'm growing so fast I don't have time" or "Cadence is just touchy-feely crap" or "My employees know what our culture is; I don't need to tell them" are excuses—and often famous last words. When a company fails to have a cadence, borrows a cadence so it looks and feels the way it *thinks* it should, or gets stuck in past cadences inherited from years or generations past, it becomes less accountable to its employees and customers and thus less meaningful and authentic to them.

LET YOUR PEOPLE FLOW—FROM YOU!

It doesn't matter if you are Steve Jobs or Bill Gates, Hugh Hefner or Larry Flynt, Richard Branson or James Dyson . . . each personalities who are famous for thinking big and acting bigger. These people don't just own who they are; they own everything that stems from who they are. They may be the most famous examples, but none of them inherited their success; they all started small and built businesses that followed their own cadence. They made sure their people—and by extension their customers—bought into and followed that cadence.

> *Cadence reflects your authenticity and accountability in acting bigger.*

James Dyson is maybe my favorite example of the six leaders I just listed. He took an award-winning idea he had as a young engineer—a wheelbarrow that used a ball instead of a wheel—and parlayed it into a business that eventually produced his eponymous bagless vacuum cleaner. He took on Hoover, and after years of struggling to find distribution, finally won. And how did he sell it? In the simplest way possible: in ads with him standing in front of a white screen using the vacuum cleaner and explaining why it was different.

If you had told me a composed British engineer explaining unique vacuum cleaner technology could successfully connect with customers and challenge a giant like Hoover (which at one point tried to rip off his technology and lost in court), I'd have said it was amazing but not surprising. Everything about Dyson's cadence felt authentic and real and extended to his product, which reflected his look and feel. The vacuum took off against a nameless and faceless Hoover and sold incredibly well despite carrying a substantially higher price tag—all because the customers connected through James Dyson to his product and the cadence of the company. But even a company like Dyson can't succeed in the long run if the cadence does not extend to its people. Retention of the best people is essential to most businesses, and cadence is a major factor in that retention. Sure, people leave for better offers or reasons you can't control, but what is making them stay before that? Cadence ties them to more than a name.

Since I called cadence a company's energy, I'll use an example from the energy industry to explain what I mean: Matthew Lanfear, the CEO of Great Eastern Energy (GEE) in New York City, an alternative energy provider focused mostly in the Northeast, grew from $5 million in revenues in 1999 to more than $300 million today despite being in an industry rife with competitors, all by leveraging his people as the point of difference and developing a system that valued them.

As Matt told me, the energy marketing industry is very easy to get into, and since every company has energy as a big part of its budget, companies will listen to anyone who claims they can save them more. "But to really be an energy marketer and an alternative supplier and do it right, you have got to have a lot of good people who know what they are doing and can do that over and over and over again year after year, and we have been able to do that," says Matt. What GEE promised instead was longevity, trust, and core competencies and sold that to customers. But to do that, the company had to retain its salespeople to deliver on that promise.

For GEE, trust was key, turnover was the enemy, and cadence was the answer. Matt created a culture at GEE that reflected his company promise. While GEE's competitors focused on growth, GEE fostered the same deep relationships with its salespeople that it wanted those salespeople to have with their customers. Commissions were structured to pay out the maximum every year (100 percent after the first year is exceptional at almost every company), and communication was constant. As a result, the salespeople stayed deeply connected to the numbers they did for GEE for any month, quarter, and year and communicated that to the customer regularly.

"It took time, and as a result we did not grow as fast," Matt says, but the trust paid off and even led to much faster growth when the company broke into the electric business in 2010: "We focused on gas and built our reputation on gas. Then we knew we could jump into electric, because we had built that trust factor with our gas base. We went from selling 10,000 kilowatt-hours of electricity when we started to 380 million four years later. By waiting, by being honest and telling people what we could and could not do and drawing on our reputation for committing to our customers and our people, word got around that we aren't schmucks."

Simply put, defining, maintaining, and refining your cadence—and the culture and systems it creates—keeps your company accountable and authentic to everyone it touches, especially your greatest points of difference: you and your people.

Wait, did I just say your systems are connected to your authenticity in thinking and acting bigger? You bet your ass I did. If you want specifics, I've discussed and outlined specific systems in my previous books. This book and chapter are about *why* you need them, not *what* you need. The important thing now is to know you need systems and standard operating procedures for everything you do to be really effective in your business:

- How you record everything from customer orders and information
- Training manuals for new employees AND those moving up in rank and responsibility, including HR documents and instructions
- Systems for dress codes, meetings, email, answering the phone, using social media . . . anything that can and must be standardized so employees understand them and don't spend any unnecessary time focusing on them

> ➤ Evaluations and disciplinary actions against employees

Disciplined systems keep your cadence from flowing out of control and undoing the focus you worked so hard to create in the last chapter. But remember: You and your people must buy into it, because your business is an extension of you. Like you, it will evolve. How I record things has changed dramatically in just the past decade. I used to walk around with tons of files, and today I hardly carry anything. Whatever way you systematize is fine, just own the systems and focus on them, or they not only will not work but their absence will fuel your inability to stay connected to all aspects of your business as you grow.

LESSONS LEARNED: DEVELOP YOUR OWN FLOW

Every business draws its energy from its cadence. Cadence is like karma— it is neither bad nor good; it just "is." Cadence is your company's river— its culture and systems—and the more it flows positively in a way that works for your company, the more it flows through anyone it touches, from employees to vendors to customers. You must develop and focus this flow as it supports and guides you through the process of thinking big and acting bigger. To develop the right cadence, start by ensuring your look and feel is genuinely yours:

> ➤ What your company looks like and how it acts reflects the culture of your organization.
> ➤ You don't need a particular feel for something to work—as long as it works for who you are and you are in control.
> ➤ Everyone who works for you must feel and buy into your cadence—including you as the leader.
> ➤ You bet your ass your systems are connected to your authenticity in thinking and acting bigger: They keep you and your company accountable and authentic.

I cannot stress how essential it is that you understand this last point for the sake of the people who work for you. Does your business have a cadence that reflects who you are? Simply put, no business is unique. Every business has just three points of difference—you, your people, and your cadence—and the systems and culture that stem from your cadence have a deep and disproportionate effect on the morale of your people—and you.

CHAPTER SIX

CLean YOUR OWN BaTHROOM

Stay Grounded and Connected

have watched episodes of CBS' *Undercover Boss* since it debuted following the Super Bowl in 2010. The show has followed dozens of executives from companies such as 7-Eleven, NASCAR, and Norwegian Cruise Line as they don disguises and work low-level jobs in their businesses to discover how they are really working. The first to sign up was Larry O'Donnell, CEO of Waste Management, who starred in the Super Bowl episode. Waste Management is a respected company and O'Donnell seemed like a good guy, but he could not stand up to the everyday demands of trash pickup. He not only performed poorly, but also chafed under some of the rules his managers enforced—rules he ostensibly put into place as CEO! He was summarily fired.

> *Focus continually on the good of your company from the bottom up or prepare to learn in a very public way just how out of touch you are.*

After revealing the ruse, O'Donnell changed the rules he found so onerous. Employees applauded the result, as did audiences and critics who loved the show. It was great TV founded on a bad business decision that can eventually undermine any company as it strives to think big, act bigger, and grow.

Leaders should not need to wait for their companies to be called by CBS to remind them to stay in touch with their businesses from the bottom up. I'm not saying that O'Donnell is a bad man or a poor businessman for losing touch with the day-to-day operations of his company, or that leaders need to pick up their "garbage" all the time to focus on the good of the company. I am, however, using this example to pose a question to you before we move any further in this book:

How can you expect people to do the things you want them to do if you won't do them, haven't done them, don't know them well enough to understand what needs to be done, or are completely disconnected from them?

Honestly, I am most leery of the leaders who won't do the day-to-day work and who shun or look down on the people who do. Don't get me wrong: Your time must be used wisely. I want leaders to do things that make them most effective in thinking big and acting bigger—that's why we need great people to help us, and you can't stay on top of everything your employees do all the time, nor should you. But that doesn't give you license to create an "ivory tower" within your business. Most jobs must be below your pay grade, but you cannot be so far above them all the time that you never look below. You can't view any work or people connected to your business—those who work for and with you as well as your customers—as figurative "garbage." To do so undermines the cadence of the company you just worked hard to develop and the trust of the people for whom you are ultimately responsible.

Stay grounded, centered, and know how things work and what is going on top to bottom in your company. You still need to remember what it is like to get your hands dirty—to stay connected to the work of the entire business so no one can ever think that you aren't. That's not just the mark of a great entrepreneur; it's the mark of a great leader.

CALL ME MR. CLEAN, NOT JOHNNY VEGAS

In my first book, *The Mirror Test*, I wrote about my battles with "Johnny Vegas Syndrome"—the evil outgrowth of success characterized by an *Ocean's 11* attitude: exaggerated swagger, excessive celebration, unbearably inflated ego, metaphorical swinging of chains, and undignified belief that you are bigger than yourself and the community that surrounds you. A crippling business disorder, it strikes leaders following periods of sustained growth or after major triumphs. The only known cure is a metaphorical slap in the face or failure.

I still struggle now and then with Johnny Vegas Syndrome, but I have learned to control it for the sake of my marriage. Sadly, as evidenced by *Undercover Boss* and the countless company failures I am constantly asked to comment on by national news organizations, my larger efforts to combat Johnny Vegas Syndrome and similar "diseases" in business have fallen short of eliminating their scourge. So I have to keep running "public service announcements" like these:

Thinking big and acting bigger requires balance as you relentlessly push forward— stay grounded and centered.

> *The only way to keep it at bay is for leaders to remember to pick up the garbage now and then. The other way eventually leads to inauthenticity, losing touch, and eventually going from growth to gone. So clean your own bathroom!*

Yes, I actually clean the bathroom at our New York City office. I do it as a reminder to keep getting my hands dirty and to never see any work as demeaning or beneath anybody—and to stand as an example to everyone in my companies as a result. It's a stake in the ground, and a visible one at that: If I am willing to take responsibility for and do the most disgusting jobs, who can complain about taking out the garbage (literally or figuratively)? Who can complain when I say, "Clean up your desk"?

When was the last time you walked the floor of one of your businesses? Picked up the phone and talked to an important vendor or customer? Ate in the cafeteria or ate your lunch at a communal table? Read and reviewed the systems, rules, or operating manual for your company? Sat and talked with people in your office who are normally filtered by your direct reports or assistants, not because you had to or for a review but just to listen? For far too many people, the answer is: "almost never."

Simply put, I am who I am (authentic) and own who I am (accountable). I own what I do and ask people to do and always have: Clean shit up. A product like Poo-Pourri can mask the scent of what drops in the bowl, but it can't hide what is left behind. Don't be the Poo-Pourri of your organization. I'm not saying you shouldn't fire yourself from certain jobs or delegate things as you grow. I'm saying don't put it off, put it down, push it off, or expect others to do everything. Clean. Shit. Up.

I have metaphorically "cleaned my bathroom" everywhere I have worked, and you should, too. The following short sections detail the ways I clean the bathroom every day. Try these. You'll find that once you do, they become an integral part of your personal corporate culture.

Connect

I send my own emails, texts, and updates—often individually, not blasts. All my social media posts come from me and nearly all are posted by me. I even write my own thank-you notes and letters.

Immerse and Attack

At my Team Logic franchise years ago, I found the systems were not working. Rather than assign the task to one of my direct reports or hire a consultant, I became an expert in those systems myself. I shopped my company as a customer to test the front desk and sales teams. I went through every part of the business to understand where the problems were and how to fix them so I knew not only what needed to be done but also that it could be done.

Stay Visible and Get "Out There"

At Kodak, I walked the halls to meet everyone I could, from the account executives down to the janitors—to understand what was really happening and hear what I needed to hear unfiltered by those who answered directly to me. Beyond the office, I went into Best Buys and put on its blue shirt to sell Kodak's printers to learn what it took to do so, ensure it was being done right, and refine any missteps.

By doing these things everywhere I go, I have stayed connected bottom to top in the businesses I have worked for and with, reinforced trust with employees and colleagues, and become an elephant that never forgets what it's like at the bottom of the ladder. Does that mean I won't fail or fall victim to a Johnny Vegas-like business syndrome? Of course not—I'm human! Does it demean me in some people's eyes? Perhaps. Haters gonna hate. But few ever think I am *above* the process even though I don't want to see or be involved in most of it anymore. And Mr. TYCO notwithstanding, fewer still would say I don't understand things and fail to push forward in everything I do.

SHOW, DON'T TELL

My goal is to get the team to own their corporate lives, clean their bathrooms too, and take on the toughest and dirtiest tasks so they can learn from them. Nothing makes me happier than when I push past an excuse to bigger thinking and action to prove the value of staying grounded and centered. Many people still recognize me from my appearance on NBC's *The Celebrity Apprentice* as part of my work at Kodak. But I was not handed the opportunity to be on the show: I made the call that got us on there—not because I had to but to show that it was *possible*!

I wanted to sell Kodak's new inkjet printer by getting it in front of a large audience. I wanted something iconic and "water cooler" worthy, because Kodak had been off the map for so long. The team mentioned having Kodak sponsor a challenge on *The Celebrity Apprentice* for the contestants.

"Great idea. We should just call Trump and get it done," I said.

Too many people think it's difficult to meet and get ahold of people, so they just don't do it. My belief is you can reach anybody, and a large part of that is because I clean my own bathroom; I know everyone poops. Famous people are still people. Usually, it's the people around the people who are the difficult ones, and rightly so: They are tasked with being protective. It might take time for me to connect, but I am going to be relentless until I do. Yet my team did not believe the same as me.

"We can't," the team said, reflecting my failure to fully extend my "because I can" attitude. "Donald Trump is too hard to reach and will never pick up the phone."

This is exactly what most people *would* think, because they have been conditioned to think that way, not because of any evidence or prior failure. It's just another convenient excuse for not doing the work, not believing in the work, and not thinking Donald Trump is grounded enough to listen.

"Yes, we can," I said.

"How are we supposed to get ahold of him?"

"I don't know." So I picked up the phone, called information, and got the number for the Trump Organization. I got his assistant and left a message designed to move Donald Trump off the fence and away from no: "Tell Mr. Trump I have a million dollars I need to spend in the next hour, and I want to know if he wants me to spend it with him or one of his competitors."

Fifteen minutes later, Trump called me back, and after a few conversations Kodak ended up on the premiere season of *The Celebrity Apprentice*. The show even let us pick the episode we wanted to be on. Can you do this if you are not the CMO of Kodak with $1 million to spend? Probably not with Trump, but that's just about scale. Money was the bottom line for Trump, but it is not the bottom line for everyone. Here is the bottom line for everyone:

You aren't going to move anyone with your pitch if you don't have the attitude that anything is possible, believe what you can do, and then deliver a message that connects both to your story and the story of who or what you are pitching.

The last point is easiest to understand: When you pitch anything, your message needs to move the audience off the fence from "maybe" or away from "no." I needed to appeal to Trump in some way—to make it about him. But the power of that message starts by asking yourself:

- ➤ What do you have to offer?
- ➤ What is the biggest thing you could do with the money you have?
- ➤ What would push you beyond what you have now that completely makes a statement about who and what you are?

Asking and answering these questions requires you to channel the power of irrational thinking we discussed in Chapter 3: Your belief should be that what you have is the best and that you will do anything to separate it from your competitors to make big things happen.

My question is: When you are ready to make things happen, do you make the call? Do you make the big move, or do you leave it in the hands of someone else—not because that someone is ready to take over cleaning the bathroom for you (because they are and can), but because you won't do the work to connect?

THE PERILS OF DISCONNECTION

Today, Barefoot Wine is the number-one wine brand in the United States. It didn't start out that way. Initially, co-founders Michael Houlihan and Bonnie Harvey thought that because they had an award-winning wine at a great price with a clever label and name people would remember and pronounce easily that it would sell "like hotcakes." It didn't. Not at all. It took some time to figure out why. Turns out they weren't just in the wine business; they were in the distribution management business, too. They thought they just had to get the wine out there and the distributors would distribute it and the retailers would sell it.

But that simply wasn't true. As Michael says today, "We could have been selling hammers, and we would have failed for the same reason:

THINK BIG ACT BIGGER

We could not get it to the general public. We had to stop thinking it was someone else's responsibility and ours was the wine. We stopped being in denial and arguing about who was doing what wrong and learned how to do it *ourselves*." And not just learn it, adds Bonnie: "We had to understand it, relate to it. We had to learn everyone's job and how they were doing it—and then physically do it. Everyone who touches your product is responsible for something you need them to do. As cute as the label was, as great as the price was, and as fine as the wine was, that was not what made it sell—keeping it on the shelf and getting it there was what made it sell."

Answer me again: Who cleans your bathroom?

Michael and Bonnie's story poses an essential question for us at this point in our story: How connected are you with all parts of your business?

If you don't know, then you are disconnected. There is no single best way to clean your bathroom; the only wrong way is to consciously or unconsciously refuse to do it.

Deidre Siegel created PEAR Core Solutions Inc., a human capital management company, in 2003 to address this very problem. She spent 17 years studying consumer behavior at companies like NBC, Time Warner, and GE Capital when she realized there were more interesting challenges inside them and decided to start her own business to address those human capital issues in companies of all sizes. "At the end of the day, you have the owners and shareholders who want to make more money, and hopefully they care about their customers, but do they really know what is going on inside their own unique business cultures?" she says. "Do they even consider or understand this culture as they recruit the talent? They must make all of that pure, raw, and real. Your people determine the culture, yet so many companies are disconnected from this. They refuse to show any empathy or engage and figure out if their people are engaged with the goals of the company and if its goals are their goals."

That's not only right but also matters for everyone at a company who cares about who they are, from the broom closet to the boardroom. You can tell when your people care like that. They have a swagger that

84   ◄   PART TWO / FOCUS IT!

says, "I know I am the best at what I do. I care." That same swagger translates directly to your customers, your cadence, and you. But what usually happens instead? As Deidre notes, many of her clients spend millions on the latest processes and systems but then do not integrate their people with them. "Who has time to think about the integration of the people, especially when you are growing in size?" she says. "A complete disconnect results."

In my work running the C-Suite Network, my capacity as columnist for *Entrepreneur* magazine (www.entrepreneur.com/author/jeffrey-hayzlett), and my appearances as a marketing analyst on Bloomberg, MSNBC, Fox Business, and others, I have been fed a steady stream of corporate mishaps to consider. Many of them come down to that same disconnection—a lack of awareness on the part of the leadership to be connected or stay connected once they engaged, even after working with someone like Deidre. Again, it is not just the jerks that this happens to. It can be folks like former Waste Management CEO Larry O'Donnell, who failed in his low-level work on *Undercover Boss*—family men with good hearts. Okay, a few assholes, too. But even the assholes must know the importance of connection from top to bottom.

When Abercrombie & Fitch's CEO Michael Jeffries retired in 2014, I was not sorry to see him go. He was no one I wanted to work for—nor would he want me. He famously courted controversy by saying larger people were not his customer base and he didn't want them shopping in his store. As a result, Abercrombie & Fitch's stores never carried sizes larger than "large," or size 10. Plus-sized people like me were a minus to him.

Many saw Jeffries' departure as validation that his prejudice had finally caught up to him. Maybe so: Sales were way off when he stepped down. But Jeffries had also led the company to massive success for more than 20 years—exceptional in CEO years. He never failed to own what he said right down to the store level. He didn't want to make bigger or older people feel good; he wanted young, attractive, thin people to feel beautiful. He exclusively pictured them in catalogs and on the website, and he hired them to work in the stores. His customers saw themselves in the brand. This exclusionary approach connected with consumers and worked for a very long time. It is entirely possible that, like an all-star athlete, Jeffries simply knew his game had declined, and it was time for him to go before he hurt the brand he loved—that his statement about his departure was completely honest: "I believe now is the right time for new leadership to take the company forward in the next phase of its development."

Again, I didn't like Jeffries' approach. I think he had issues, and not just because he had his plane spritzed with the Abercrombie & Fitch scent and piped in Phil Collins music. He had his own style, and those were his creature comforts. But no one could deny he was aware of what was going on at the company and seemed to embrace and connect to it all. He was never going to literally clean his own bathroom, but he knew who did, which is more than I can say for some companies and some CEOs.

Contrast Abercrombie & Fitch with another clothing company: Lululemon. The Vancouver, British Columbia–based brand took a major hit in 2013 when its popular Luon™ fabric yoga pants were found to be see-through and it had to implement a massive recall, which cost it about $67 million and an endless stream of snickers. Some say it also cost then-CEO Christine Day her job—that she stepped down before she could be fired. I disagree. Day was grounded and centered in her job before and during the controversy. She understood the faux pas and moved in all the right ways to make sure the damage was short-term, handling it swiftly and well. She acknowledged the mistake, implemented the recall, and fired the product officer responsible for overseeing the pants—exactly the action you would expect from a CEO who had been with the company for more than five years, had stayed deeply connected to it and its success, and knew the value of loyal customers. The company stock had grown more than twentyfold in her tenure. Stores were opening everywhere. Shareholders and employees loved her. Whatever was going on, Day knew who cleaned her bathroom at Lululemon.

I can't say the same for Chip Wilson, the founder and chairman of Lululemon. I get that some would say Wilson is, for lack of a better word, crazy. Google "Chip Wilson crazy quotes" and you'll see what

I mean. But crazy gave way to disconnected when Lululemon ran into another kerfuffle shortly after the see-through pants ordeal: Its yoga pants were pilling on the thighs. Rather than owning the new mistake and handling it the way Day did, Wilson gave an interview on Bloomberg in which he blamed the customers, saying, "[S]ome women's bodies just don't actually work for [Lululemon yoga pants]. It's really about the rubbing through the thighs, how much pressure is there over a period of time, how much they use it."

True? Maybe. Smart, grounded, and connected to his brand? Not.

Lululemon isn't Abercrombie & Fitch. It's connected to fitness and the fast-growing world of yoga, with its spiritual origins, peaceful approach, and welcoming nature to all. You'd expect the founder of a company like that to say something like this when it came to the pilling: "Women should look and feel great when they work out, and we have to do a better job." But no, he decides to blame women's thighs. Yes, he *was* calling you fat. Women, not just Lululemon customers, rightly took offense. I heard him say this live on Bloomberg, but while others were getting their pilled knickers in a twist, I also heard an even more amazingly catastrophic answer he gave to a follow-up question by the Bloomberg host: Should he come back and be the CEO? Wilson's response: "I mean, quite frankly, we're maybe too wealthy now."

THE DANGERS OF LOSING PERSPECTIVE

In those words of Chip Wilson lie the true perils of disconnection and lost perspective. Wilson had completely lost touch, the way Day or Jeffries had not. When he resigned as chairman at the end of 2013 (and then from the board of directors in 2015), no one doubted why. You could argue that Wilson was just being himself and selling it like it is: Every baby is not pretty! Every child is not a sports star! Every woman is not suited to our yoga pants! I agree with a selling-it-like-it-is approach, but this wasn't like that. It was like *Wilson*.

> *Disconnection is a lonely island of entitlement in business.*

You may think you're acting bigger, but all you're doing is inflating your ego and losing perspective. That ego and its inability to overcome the power of real connections was never on better display in the fight that nearly tore apart Market Basket, a beloved New England grocery chain. Owned by the Demoulas family since the original store opened in 1917, Market Basket had overcome family squabbles in the past but had never experienced anything like the fight between the families of the original owner's sons—George and Mike—in 2014. Mike's side wanted to invest more in the business; George's side wanted to take more money out in dividends. All efforts for one side to buy out the other failed until eventually George's side gained control of the board and quickly fired the CEO, their cousin, Arthur T. Demoulas, who was on Mike's side and deeply beloved by the workers.

Market Basket is famous for treating its employees well, which had yielded decades of deep loyalty and excellent customer service to go with its quality food at low prices. So what happened next was perhaps not surprising but was still stunning for its sustained outrage and solidarity with the ousted CEO: The employees walked out and stayed out, protesting at the stores and taking their case to the people and media. Market Basket tried everything from threats of termination to hosting job fairs, and nothing worked. Shoppers stayed away to support the workers. Vendors stayed away, too. Few if any spoke in support of George's family, which controlled the store. The company lost tens of millions of dollars over six weeks as the squabble played out in store parking lots, boardrooms, and the media, until Mike's side brought in outside investors and forced George's side to accept their buyout.

That's the power of connection that we have discussed in this chapter. Boston.com said as much in naming Market Basket's workers its 2014 "Bostonians of the Year": "The 25,000 employees—many with decades of service and working alongside their husbands, mothers, sons, aunts—showed incredible devotion to a boss and remarkable stamina and determination. They knew their pay and benefits were unmatched in today's cutthroat world of retail and gambled that if they stuck to their protests, they could emerge victorious. They caught the attention of customers, governors, U.S. labor secretaries past and present, CEOs and business scholars from all over. When the company sale was announced in late August and employees returned to work, the joy was contagious. People who had never shopped a Market Basket before just had to visit to see what the fuss was about."

Listen, I get it. Balance is hard to achieve when you're "pedal to the metal." You need to push forward but have to stay grounded. Like the play between being rational and irrational, cleaning your bathroom is a dance. Truth and authenticity hang in the balance. Where they intersect is a great spot as long as you don't lose that perspective, and we all lose perspective sometimes. It can happen innocently enough. I often tell the story of meeting my wife's great-grandmother, Grand Agnes, for the first time. Grand Agnes stood 4'10" on a good day. I'm 6'3." Grand Agnes looked up at me and then turned to my wife and said, "Isn't he bigger than necessary?" It was not until years later, when I saw a picture of myself with my rugby team, that I realized, while I am not bigger than necessary, I am *big*. Of course, I played big and had a healthy ego, but until I saw that photo, I always thought I was the same size as or smaller than the other guys. I thought I was just acting bigger, but I was a head taller than my teammates. What made me think I was smaller than I was?

I learned that day just how easy it is to lose your sense of perspective on or in any "field," especially if you rest on who you have been—if you have failed to focus on what matters, stayed thoughtful, and listened to the voices of your

> *Remember: Everyone poops.*

employees and customers. The consequences will cost you in the next part of this book, especially when it comes to the biggest obstacles and the need to be in a constant state of awareness of who you are, how you are perceived, the trends in your industry, and how you (and your competitors) are doing things.

You can never be too big or moving too fast to engage on this level. Consider what Matt Preschern, executive vice president and CMO of HCL Technologies, a rapidly growing multibillion-dollar Indian global IT services company, told me in an interview in front of my conference of C-Suite executives: "I personally believe the word 'relationship' is overstated. Too many companies go back into a transaction mode when the contract itself should be the beginning of the relationship. Salespeople sell, but we believe that most of our customer touch points are not with our salespeople but the teams that are with our customers day in and day out after the salespeople have finished."

To empower its employees in these relationships, HCL created a program called LeadGen, in which every employee can record and bring forward ideas on how to improve what the company does. The best ones are rewarded on a regular basis. "From a business perspective, this has led to more than $500 million in new ideas that frontline employees are creating," says Matt. "For our 100,000 employees, this has created a culture of 'ideapreneurship.' It is not enough for a company to say, 'We have to empower our employees.' We have to give them the opportunity to raise their voices. We also have an internal employee branding team that is fully engaged in our intranet, which does all sorts of fun things for recruiting young employees. We have monthly meetings in every part of the world to maintain this—and the marketing department as well as HR runs the entire program. That's the part that is different from my experience: Our employees are part of the culture. If you believe in the concept that your employees are your biggest brand ambassadors externally, what makes you think that the ones who are defining the brand promise externally shouldn't be the ones who help empower the ones who deliver it? Then they have the power and the ability to act."

Okay, maybe you don't have the resources like HCL to do this, but is your connection to your people strong enough to even take the first step? How do you know you have gotten disconnected, entitled, detached?

When you not only believe your poop doesn't stink, but also that you don't even poop.

This is why every time I watch ABC's *Shark Tank*, I am never surprised at the reason the vast majority of pitches fall apart: the valuations of the business. I love the big thinking and in some cases bigger action that has gotten the businesses and inventors in front of the Sharks. I like that they believe their business can and will make the millions upon tens of millions they have yet to make, if only the Sharks will bite. But those words must be backed up by something more than belief, attitude, promises, and a few months or quarters of sales. They must be grounded in reality, too. Those that aren't are always proved to be so much air by the Sharks.

This is also why I can always tell the ones who will get an offer. They stand up and know they are being a little irrational, but they never really lose perspective. They might not be ready for what they are asking, but they are ready to try. I see myself in them: Smart, regular people going all in who had to think bigger and act bigger to get there, knowing they still have to do so much more. They are grounded and connected, cleaning their bathrooms and doing it all—and ready to face the obstacles ahead. But it never hurts, just in case, to pick up a copy of the children's book *Everyone Poops*.

LESSONS LEARNED: CLEAN YOUR OWN BATHROOM

CBS' *Undercover Boss* is an entertaining and important reminder about just how easy it is to lose perspective on and connection to your business and discover just how out of touch you are. Most of us, however, won't have that TV show to help us find our way. We need to take it on ourselves to remember what it is like to get our hands dirty—to stay connected to the work of the entire business. That's not just the mark of a great entrepreneur; it's the mark of a great leader.

> ➤ Don't expect your people to do the things you want them to do if you won't do them, haven't done them, don't know them well enough to understand what needs to be done, or are completely disconnected from them.
>
> ➤ Connect and immerse yourself in your business. Attack problems by understanding them yourself, stay visible, and get "out there" to stay grounded in all parts of your business.
>
> ➤ Disconnection is a lonely island of entitlement in business—it's a dance, but you must find balance between pushing forward and staying grounded.
>
> ➤ Remember: Everyone poops—keep your perspective!

I know perspective is tough when moving at the speed of business today. Like the play between being rational and irrational, cleaning your bathroom means dancing between pushing forward and staying grounded. But you must learn the steps to that dance. Focus continually on the good of your company from the bottom up: Stay grounded and connected, and clean your own bathroom!

PART THREE

MAKE IT

HAPPEN!

CHAPTER SEVEN

STEAMROLL OBSTACLES AND ENEMIES
Think Differently!

"**W**e don't work with assholes."

That was the first slide Mark Wolfe and LeVar Burton of RRKidz Inc., home of the beloved *Reading Rainbow* franchise, put up for their audience at a conference of entrepreneurs. I was keynoting at the same conference and had met Mark and LeVar in the green room before they went onstage. We all felt an instant connection beyond speaking, *Reading Rainbow* (which my kids watched), and LeVar's celebrity. They asked if I would watch their presentation, something I rarely have the time (or honestly the desire) to do. For them, I sat in the front row, and their first slide not only made me like them even more, but also further explained why I felt such a connection.

In just five words, Mark and LeVar had stated quite clearly who they were, where they wanted to go, *and* the main obstacle they faced.

You might be forgiven for thinking RRKidz would have welcomed working with anyone, including assholes, considering the status of *Reading Rainbow* at the time. After 23 years, PBS had pulled the show that had helped a generation of children love reading, and Mark and LeVar were striving to bring it back for future generations. They knew an audience existed for *Reading Rainbow*, if only because of the huge parent response to the show's demise. The connection to *Reading Rainbow* ran so deep, LeVar told me, that people were more likely to sing the show's theme song when they saw him than call him Geordi (his *Star Trek: The Next Generation* character). People had placed their trust in the show and wanted *Reading Rainbow* to be what Mark and LeVar call the "Netflix for kids' books."

But re-launching *Reading Rainbow* on a new platform was an expensive proposition—at least $1 million. For two years, RRKidz had looked for traditional funding in the venture capital community to no avail. LeVar's name and their brand's familiarity coupled with empirical research that said this would succeed attracted interest, but not the *right* interest. Mark and LeVar wanted to build a *Reading Rainbow* for the long term. Assholes or anyone without an equal stake in that were not welcome, and that made money harder to find. As Mark says, "VCs have a very specific return strategy that they have to offer to the people that have funded them, and we were not interested in building a company and flipping it in a few months."

That's how profound Mark and LeVar's responsibility and accountability to *Reading Rainbow* were. They were willing to pass up the easy money to find the right money. I know people *say* words like "accountability" and "responsibility" all the time, but on that day, and when I interviewed them myself as part of my C-Suite Network Conference in Los Angeles in 2014 (http://c-suitetv.com/video/executive-perspectives-rrkidz/), I knew those words really meant something to them. What struck me was the emotion I got to see up close: LeVar's eyes watering when he talked about his mother and the love of reading she instilled in him; their pulses quickening when they talked about future possibilities; the thoughtfulness that suffused every answer and reflected their genuine bond with the *Reading Rainbow* community. They felt a duty to the children, parents, and teachers who had made *Reading Rainbow* so successful. They were guardians of the trust.

To recap, RRKidz had everything we have covered so far regarding thinking big and acting bigger:

- ➤ Doing it "because I can"? Check.
- ➤ Owning your story—who you are and what you are in it for—with deep, abiding passion? Check.
- ➤ Being a little pigheaded and irrational in pushing forward—no excuses? Check.
- ➤ Laser-like focus on what they needed? Check.
- ➤ Deep connection to the community? Double check.

Mark and LeVar had the tools they needed to make their future happen. They just hadn't reaped the rewards yet. To do so, they needed to steamroll one admittedly huge obstacle by thinking differently. The solution? Crowdfunding. Turning to their greatest strength—people who wanted the show back—to help bring it back, Mark and LeVar chose Kickstarter as their platform for the project, created everything they needed from videos to incentives, reached out to their community, and pressed "go." When their Kickstarter ended in July 2014, 105,857 backers had pledged more than $5.4 million, which became more than $6.4 million when Seth MacFarlane, creator of *Family Guy* on Fox TV and one-time Oscar host, contributed an additional $1 million. At the time, it was the biggest Kickstarter ever in terms of number of backers and, as of this book's going to press, was still in the top ten overall in money raised and number of backers.

"The Kickstarter was such a miraculous event for us because our backs were against it," adds LeVar. "One of the biggest obstacles for us was the funding. Kickstarter gave us the rocket fuel that we were looking for, and now we are a 31-year-old startup!"

"I suppose like everybody else, we were a business, and we followed the traditional business approach to funding," says Mark. "Kickstarter didn't exist when *Reading Rainbow* went off PBS. Our idea worked when we broke away from traditional approaches and then cut through the noise of Kickstarter. Sure, we had an advantage between LeVar's name and the *Reading Rainbow* to getting discovered. That's a huge obstacle for any business today—discovery—and we needed more than most businesses to get started. But in the end, our seed funding came from long-term players: the people. That is why it was the most backed Kickstarter ever: the people."

In the end, Mark and LeVar's obstacle wasn't funding; funding was the problem, and thinking was the obstacle. There are other crowdfunding sites and options like the direct public offering, and I have heard that they are becoming more popular with minorities, who are often shut out from VC funding. They also generate immediate direct connection and responsibility to customers and early adopters, as well as marketing and media coverage when they break through. The success of Pebble, the smartwatch company that raised more than $10 million in its first Kickstarter in 2012 for its second gen watch and then more than $20 million in 2015 for the latest version, will be a topic of conversation for years. (They even included a bulk package for resellers to develop retail relationships.)

What's your obstacle, and what do you need to get through it, around it, or remove it to make big things happen?

But regardless of your situation, the point is to get beyond traditional thinking and approach the funding differently, which is why it is so important to follow the lessons in Chapter 3 before starting the steps here. All of us have overcome obstacles to get where we are, but it is being able to use what we have learned to steamroll *ongoing* obstacles that takes us to the next level again and again. The only way to do that is to put the obstacles front and center. This is a bit like addressing the elephant in the room, but I prefer to look at them another way: as bullies that stand in the doorway to thinking big and acting bigger. The best way to overcome a bully? Calm him down. The best way to deal with obstacles? Calm down and say exactly what the obstacle is.

A lot of times we simply don't identify what the obstacles are. The result is often complacency and inaction. We try to avoid the bully. We pretend the bully isn't there and then go through a different doorway that leads to a smaller story. This happens in too many companies, and as a result their leaders get caught in a version of the movie *Groundhog Day*, in which Bill Murray's character keeps living the same day over and over until he gets it right. But they'll never get it right by thinking and acting small. Some might be getting closer that way, but most are just living the old definition of crazy: repeating the same thing over and over and expecting a different result.

The good news is that if you've truly done the work you needed to do to get here, those obstacles present only opportunities to think differently and thus bigger—the first step in making things happen.

To inspire you and show what I mean, let's look at some ways everyday companies steamrolled obstacles to success—the questions they asked and the actions they took to disrupt and flatten those obstacles, from conventional wisdom to the competition. The examples, like RRKidz, offer self-contained lessons, including one about the importance of enemies in thinking big and acting bigger. But no obstacle is bigger than the bully of traditional thinking.

YOUR WAY CAN BE DRASTICALLY DIFFERENT

Jim, my writer, hates the expression "Think outside the box." I get why: What box? Why do you think there is a box? Who put you *in* a box in the first place? Boxes are the barriers and excuses we use to limit the stories we can tell. I understand what the expression means, but to me it seems like thinking outside the box is an excuse for not believing any box can be bigger. Boxes are always bigger than we think. They may have borders, but they should be expandable, adaptable, and permeable. Any borders should be like state lines, not walls. They may slow you down, but not for long. But even if you hit a wall in a box, you can attack it: Go up and over, under, or through it. When I visited the Seattle Sounders FC football club (or soccer team, for you Americans who associate football with the NFL) that plays as part of Major League Soccer (MLS), I learned there is another option for the wall: Blow it up (http://c-suitetv.com/video/seattle-sounders-csuite-with-jeffrey-hayzlett/).

"Lead your own team and people." Even if businesses outsource some services, this is the way they traditionally operate and define management. The Seattle Sounders did exactly that for the better part of two decades and failed to grow. The original Seattle Sounders team was founded in 1994 and played in the American Professional Soccer League and the United States Soccer League, and while the team had some success it never drew huge fan support. The team had tried to expand into MLS, but fan interest seemed small and the price tag high.

It wasn't until 2008, when the Sounders teamed with Joe Roth as majority owner, that they won an MLS franchise for 2009. But despite Roth's star power as a Hollywood power broker, they were still the Sounders, still in Seattle, and still selling soccer to a fan base that had never exceeded 4,500 (the capacity of its stadium). What made them think this would be different? Turns out it was football: *American* football. Enter Sounders' minority investor Paul Allen, of Microsoft fame, who owns the NFL's Seattle Seahawks. Allen suggested the Sounders and Seahawks share their management teams, merging their lifestyles and interests.

Do your own thing? Manage your own teams? For a lot of companies that works; the Sounders decided it didn't for them anymore, and Roth saw opportunity in Allen's untraditional offer. Normally, as was the case with RRKidz, tradition can blind a company to thinking differently. The Sounders avoided that trap in their new incarnation and put all the pieces together differently to fuel massive change and growth for the team, all while retaining the team's brand identity. In partnering with the Seahawks, a team with a rabid fan base and massively successful operations, the Sounders could capitalize on the same assets that made the Seahawks winners and CenturyLink Field a loud and deadly place to play for visiting teams.

Some people have asked me if this was just luck that everything fell into place when it did for the Sounders. Of course, luck plays a part when heading into uncharted business territory. The general manager of the Seattle Sounders did say it wasn't one big thing, but 20 little things that fell in line at the same time to make this unconventional arrangement work. But you can only make so much of that luck without remembering who you are *and still* truly committing to the new direction.

> *Something is only impossible until it has been done— or when you think it can't be done.*

If you're a business going through major growth, why not go to where the food is? Go talk to someone who has done this before, even if they are not exactly in your business—especially if they are not! With the biggest obstacles, always be willing to consider models different from what you have been taught or seen.

The Seahawks' experience with digital marketing, fan appreciation, and sponsorship solicitation was a major help in ensuring the Sounders didn't fall into the same ruts they had in the past. The combined executive team focused on skilled disciplines. While the Sounders' GM focused exclusively on building his team's product, the management of sponsorships, fan base, marketing, and more was all done in conjunction with the Seahawks. It gave the Sounders a head start in moving from being a minor league team to a major league team overnight and avoided some of the blunders they probably would have made. On every measurable level—from attendance to merchandise to team record—the result was astounding success.

Notice I wrote that last paragraph in the past tense. That's because the Sounders have separated from the Seahawks since I visited them last. They realized that they shared a stadium with the Seahawks, but their fans had only a 2 percent crossover rate. The team set MLS record attendance marks year after year and World Cup Fever built in 2014, so they took what they learned to grow even faster on their own. The Sounders used the Seahawks' help to get ahead and then flew its management nest like a baby bird that needs to think and act bigger on its own. The Sounders still play in the same stadium as the Seahawks, as no other home in Seattle could hold its rabid fan base, which remains far and away the largest in Major League Soccer. But the Sounders are attending to that base on their own. Initial results showed no drop-off: In 2014, revenue was strong and attendance was steady, exceeding capacity at the field as the team finished first in the conference and made the conference finals.

You don't need to be the Sounders or have tens of millions in annual revenue to think this unconventionally. Walter Bond is a former NBA player who is now an award-winning speaker. But his speaking career was a "brick" until he approached things differently in business. "For three years in my speaking and leadership training business, I failed to take what I knew I needed to do to succeed as a professional athlete and apply it to my business. Instead, I felt hopeless and stuck," says Walter. "Then, I realized why I had lost my mojo. I had tried to follow traditional corporate 'rules' and hated it. I needed to use the power and hope of my secret weapon as an athlete in my business: I needed an off-season.

"The off-season is when professional athletes get bigger, stronger, faster, and better at what they do, improving and developing the skills they need to pull and stay ahead of the competition and improve the quality of what they do and who they are. I learned to use my off-seasons in speaking—between Thanksgiving and New Year's—to learn to be a better speaker, connect more effectively with my audience, speak more profoundly, and thus increase my value and grow my business. That's how I had thought, executed, and dominated my dream as an athlete. To this day, year in and year out, my off-seasons are when I make good on that old maxim to 'work on your business, not in your business.' I take a step back, look at every part of my company with my people, and ask what pieces must improve: sales calls, website, product, services, marketing, branding, fee structure, systems, strategy, customer relations—anything that will help my company grow next year and continue to grow exponentially over time to dominate the competition."

The result? Since he incorporated these principles, Walter has had significant year-over-year growth. Moreover, the work *excites* his team and Walter in the same way it does professional athletes and sports teams starting a new season! All because Walter challenged convention: He disrupted the way people normally do business and changed the way that business was done.

KNOW THE POWER OF "AND"

By combining their strengths with the Seahawks, the Sounders created a completely untraditional link that used one very traditional word: "and"—one of the most effective words in the English language for eliminating and even transcending obstacles.

Russ Mann, the former CEO of Covario, which was one of the largest search engine marketing agencies in the U.S. before it was acquired in 2014, and current CMO of Nintex, the leading workflow automation software platform, told me a story about an event sponsorship his company was considering with one of its bigger partners. Russ hadn't been at the company long, but with the words of a past mentor in his head—"go big or don't go"—he listened as they discussed options: Should we be Gold? Platinum? Sponsorship prices were steep and this was a new event for the company—so do we spend the money on Platinum even though Gold is more expensive than Platinum was last year? There are two or three of these events so maybe we should do it for the next one . . . ?

Finally, Russ said, "Guys, the question is not whether we should be gold or platinum for this or the other two or three we have with this partner each year. The question is: How do we go bigger on this? We should go to this partner and say, 'We have a million-dollar check to spend on this in the future. What can we get for that? We want to commit to platinum for three years and six events. We want a discount for committing upfront and getting rid of all negotiation for these events individually.' That says to them we're not going away and you're not going away."

See all those "ands" Russ used in there? He pushed the team to go beyond the seemingly big thinking and action of spending the $150,000 or so it would cost for each event and parlayed all they could commit into one big action that got the partner's attention. They made a statement that the company was out there, thinking big, and, as Russ says, "going to win *and* always going to be at the top." According to Russ, his audacity surprised everyone, but even the CFO backed his play, knowing that the company was getting more for its money and saving time by committing to the action without paying it all upfront. "It was a complete shift in thinking," Russ adds, "and now the team is thinking big in everything they do."

> *Don't settle: Use "and" to think beyond the questions and obstacles you have now to eliminate them for the future.*

As we discussed before, too much "and" can lead to indulgence, but it can also make you see how much bigger something could be, even if you shouldn't or wouldn't normally do it that way. Consider Autodesk, a multinational software corporation. Its 3-D design software has been used for everything from the New York City Freedom Tower to the Tesla electric car to Academy Award–winning designs (http://c-suitetv.com/video/autodesk-c-suite-with-jeffrey-hayzlett/). Leading edge for sure, the company is understandably leery of getting stuck, so they keep pushing through changes. This is interesting if only because much of the team has been with the company for more than 15 years. Still, that team has adapted with the times and has updated constantly, right down to the delivery mechanism. Previously, Autodesk had seen the change from software in boxes to downloads, but now everything needed to move to the cloud. Problem was, they didn't know if their customers could follow them there.

Where a lot of software companies would say, "Okay, it's easier for us to put this on the cloud and *make* you switch," Autodesk knew their customer base well. Many of them are architects and engineers building bridges, airports, hospitals—major facilities and infrastructure items that take years to happen. They can't switch them out in the middle of the project!

What Autodesk did was use "and" to reaffirm their commitment to those customers and anticipate the obstacle before it became one: They realized that they had to offer established customers both versions of the software for a sustained period of time—and that they had to make the investment to do so. Was that costly? Absolutely, but the payoff was huge: They helped their customers make the transition *and* became even more connected to them.

Autodesk had the patience to sustain and then grow its market, and, as a result, it developed a lot of tolerance for allowing things to unfold over a longer period of time. The maturity of its people certainly worked to its advantage, too; they understood the need to be patient and to commit to their customers. But what if patience isn't a virtue? What if your commitment to a customer leads to a situation where he who hesitates is lost? Then you need a different word to steamroll your obstacle: resilience.

BE RESILIENT

Like so many entrepreneurs, Scott Jordan, the CEO of SCOTTeVEST Inc., did not go into business on his own as a first career. He was a practicing lawyer before he had the idea he nurtured into his multipocket, tech-ready clothing line (its slogan: "Our pockets, your freedom").

Not every career prepares you for the life of an entrepreneur or small-businessperson. If you can't stomach something that feels like riding the Formula Rossa roller coaster, don't bother signing up. (As of 2015, Formula Rossa was the world's fastest roller coaster. Located in Ferrari World in the United Arab Emirates, it packs 1.7G of force and goes so fast that riders have to wear safety goggles because bugs and small particles become missile-like projectiles. That's a little bit like life as a startup, only you can vomit after the roller coaster for a full recovery.) Of course, every entrepreneur knows this and faces doubts. But the story Scott told me might make those with sensitive stomachs reconsider why they are doing it, even if they consider returning to a previous career as "unimaginable" as Scott did.

Scott's obstacle found him before he even had a product to sell. It was 2001, and he had made a connection at Hammacher Schlemmer to pitch his vests. He nailed his presentation and was rewarded with a big first order: 3,000 vests. "I was in business!" says Scott. He immediately invested most of his life savings in producing those vests, which would take months to arrive from China, but he was confident in every way that they would sell the second customers saw them.

While he waited and waited for the vests to arrive, Scott followed up with Hammacher Schlemmer but started getting worried when he never heard back. What happened next will strike fear in the hearts of entrepreneurs and small-business owners everywhere: "I'm a pretty impatient guy and tend to follow up a lot, but it seemed like Hammacher wasn't returning my emails or my calls at all," Scott says. "Then I got the news: The buyer I met with was 'out,' as in, out of the company. Gone. And my order with them disappeared just as quickly. I was stuck. Actually, I was something that rhymes with 'stuck-ed.'"

Don't get mad.
Don't get even.
Just get ahead.

Scott could have folded. He could have started sending out resumes to every law firm in town. Instead, he got motivated, and what he chose to do was act bigger and get ahead.

First, Scott learned how to build a website and rechristened SCOTTeVEST as an e-commerce company. He then flew to New York City and walked from building to building to generate press, talking to anyone who would see him. Literally *anyone.* "I demoed my vest for cab drivers, airline passengers, secretaries . . . anyone who would watch me unload the 20 gadgets from my clever little vest," says Scott. "I put the vests up for pre-order and sold lots of them before the shipment even reached the U.S. I did pre-orders a decade before Kickstarter and Indiegogo!"

I'm not saying a person in Scott's situation isn't entitled to be angry (just take the anger out on inanimate objects, not people). But everyone knows a cornered animal is the most dangerous. *That fear and anger can lead to a complete shutdown where you just give up and go down blaming anyone and everything for your situation. Or you can use that fear to fight back and see possibilities you never did or never needed to when things were going well. Take responsibility for your survival.*

As Scott told me, "That level of motivation—that level of purposeful desperation—is something I still tap into. I still paint myself into corners to force myself to find the boldest way out, and my business is thriving 15 years later because of it." "Purposeful desperation"— what a great phrase that perfectly sums up the resilience we all must have in facing obstacles. It also reminds me of something I said at the beginning of this chapter that was incomplete. Remember? I said boxes are the barriers and excuses we use to limit the stories we can tell. That's true, but it doesn't mean the barriers others have set up aren't real. Sometimes it's not just "in your head." The haters are out there. You will have enemies, even if it is just good old-fashioned competition. And what I said before applies to your enemies as well: Don't get mad; don't get even; just get ahead.

WE LIVE IN STORIES AND EVERY GOOD STORY NEEDS A VILLAIN

Scott Jordan actually provides a great example of what I mean by that header when he walked away from a deal on season three of the hit ABC series *Shark Tank*. Scott fought with Mark Cuban, left $1 million on the table, and told Robert Herjavec and Kevin O'Leary *they* were "out." (In a scene that was later edited from the show, Robert refused to shake Scott's hand as he left.) "It was one of the most controversial episodes in the history of the show," says Scott. "All because I was unwilling to give them a piece of SCOTTeVEST, only the licensing of TEC-Technology Enabled Clothing®."

But there are two sides to every story. Scott actually believed that the Sharks were baiting him into talking about his SCOTTeVEST brand name on TV, not just the technology he was pitching. He refused to do that, however, because of the contract everyone signs with Sony, Mark Burnett, and ABC to be on the show. Under its terms at the time, Scott had to give options for 5 percent of his revenue or 2 percent of his profits to the show, whether he got a deal, turned a deal down, or failed to get an offer. In other words, they had an option at no cost to them to get a cut, no matter what. That's why Scott presented the TEC-Technology Enabled Clothing only.

The episode made for great TV, but I can see both sides, and Scott's side is just as compelling as the Sharks'—and underappreciated. In that

> *You should have the biggest, baddest enemy you can imagine in your space, because you want to be the biggest and baddest in that space.*

situation, with the Sharks staring down at him, I can understand how Scott felt: cornered, a little intimidated, and bullied. And in that moment he refused to be taken advantage of. So he walked. He created an "enemy" in the Sharks as a result, but in steamrolling obstacles, that is not necessarily a bad thing. The bigger they are, the more opportunity in taking them down. Don't have an enemy? Create one.

Yes, I just said create an enemy.

A lot of startups come to me and say they have this new thing and it's really good and blah, blah, blah. When they stop talking, one of the first questions I ask is, "Who else is in this space?"

"No one, that's what is so good."

"Actually, it's not that good then."

"What do you mean?"

"If you don't have anyone in that space, preferably a big bad enemy, then what's the opportunity to be the biggest and baddest? Who's the Big Bad Wolf in your story?"

There's a reason every great business success has an "enemy" to take down, and it's the same reason every great fairy tale has a villain: it makes for a great story for people to buy into. It wasn't just that Apple or Uber were bigger products and ideas—they were able to cast themselves against something that was not working (PCs and cabs, respectively). In fact, Apple has rarely been first to market with its signature products; it expanded the market for everything from digital music players to mobile phones by being the best, biggest, and baddest (whether you saw them as the villain or not).

This works for people, too. Before Michael Jordan took the NBA to the international stratosphere, Magic Johnson and Larry Bird transformed the NBA with their stardom *and* their rivalry. It wasn't enough that each was a success; they had to see the other as the ultimate obstacle—the enemy that had to be eliminated. A warrior's greatest respect is for an enemy worth fighting. Bird and Johnson drove and pushed each other. To win, they had to constantly think and act bigger and make their teammates do the same.

I wish I had applied this insight to everything in my business life and realized earlier that I'm bigger than the bullies (more than just physically), and that if pushed, I can push back. But I didn't really learn this until I was 36 years old and working for a software company in California. The people around me had tech degrees and Harvard MBAs. I had practical knowledge, street smarts, and contacts. That made me their equal, but not in the eyes of one MBA; he was smarter and better than me, yet I kept scoring. At one point he told me he was so angry at me that he wanted to punch me. I told him to go ahead, but he better knock me out because if not I was going to get up and kick his ass. That was when I decided I was not going to be bullied by people who think they're smarter than I am. From then on I did the things that I still do today and steamrolled every villain and enemy I faced.

And what happens if the other guy is the good guy? Well, then you're the villain. And that's OK, too. Mark Wolfe and LeVar Burton may not work with assholes, but lots of people do, especially if they give people what they want and never pretend to be something else. Think of coaches like Bill Belichick of the New England Patriots or Abercrombie & Fitch's CEO Michael Jeffries from the previous chapter. *You can be the villain, just not your own enemy.*

How do we avoid doing that? An easy trap to fall in is to get obsessed with the negative. So many times people get mad at things said in emails, online reviews, tweets, phone calls, and interviews, especially when they come from people you know, did business with, and maybe even trusted. I can't say I don't, but I still keep those people in my circle, especially in social media. This is in my nature. Most people think I am a real hard ass, and, at certain times, I am. I either want to seduce you or I want to kill you—those are my two modes of operation. But there are many times people have done something not nice, and I did not kill them. My question isn't "How can I bury you?" but "How can I use you?" and "How do I do this with my enemies without losing my head (or at least getting my hand bitten off)?"

Sure, sometimes I get my hand bitten off, which is a learning experience, but I still refuse to burn the bridge. I may not walk that bridge again, but I won't spend too much energy trying to get back at a person or company, or being obsessed with going negative. I don't want that energy affecting what I need to get done. Focusing on the past will only prevent me from making things happen in the future. That's creating obstacles I don't need.

LESSONS LEARNED: OBSTACLES AND ENEMIES

The examples in this chapter from companies that steamrolled obstacles to success—the questions they asked and the actions they took to disrupt and flatten those obstacles, from conventional wisdom to the competition—were designed to inspire you to steamroll the obstacles you will face as you think big and act bigger. Sure, we all have overcome obstacles to get where we are, but being able to use what we have learned so far to steamroll the *ongoing* obstacles we face will take us to the next level again and again. The only way to do that is to put the obstacles front and center.

- Know your obstacles and what it takes to go through them, go around them, or remove them to make big things happen.
- Obstacles present opportunities to think differently and thus bigger, the first step in making things happen.
- Something is only impossible when it hasn't been done or when you think it can't be done; consider models different from what you have been taught or seen.
- Don't settle: Think beyond the questions and obstacles you have now to eliminate them for the future.
- Don't get mad. Don't get even. Just get ahead. Especially when it comes to your enemies—and if you don't have an enemy, create one!

Remember: obstacles are like bullies that stand in the doorway to thinking big and acting bigger. These bullies are also enemies in our stories, and we *need* enemies to help push us forward. Every great business success needs an enemy to take down; enemies make for better stories for people to buy into.

CHAPTER EIGHT

Be in a constant state of awareness

Get Over Yourself and Know What You Don't Know

I sometimes go fishing in a remote area of Canada accessible by driving across the border to a floatplane where we meet our host, Trapper Bob. We stay in his cabin, and he regales us with stories as he eats his bacon and Oreos and drinks his scotch (the only things I have ever seen him eat and drink). Of course, Bob has other things for us to eat in his cabin, including this blueberry jam that I love. It comes in a can, and it tastes great. The first time I had it, I kept thinking, "Blueberry jam in a can! It tastes great, and it comes *in a can,* which is so unusual. And it's Canadian jam. I have never seen it in the U.S.—I need to bring home this jam!"

A couple of trips later, still smitten with the jam, I bought a case of it before we drove home. While the jam itself wasn't too expensive, I paid a fortune to ship it back to South Dakota. "Who knows how long this stuff will be around?" I thought. "I want to share it with my closest friends and family."

My wife, Tami, saw the case of jam when it arrived, gave me the "Jeff-what-the . . ." look, and then asked, "Why did you do that?"

"Sweetheart, you don't understand," I said. "This is the best jam *in the world.* It's unbelievable and it comes *in a can* and you can *only* get it in Canada. It's really special and I don't know how much they're going to make anymore. We are going to keep 12 cans for us and give the rest away as special presents."

Tami said nothing, and over the next couple of weeks I kept my promise, doling out a can apiece to relatives over the holidays like it was caviar, telling each one the story about where the jam comes from and how special it is. Tami mocked me every time I did, but she didn't understand. I *knew* how special this jam was.

Soon after I had started handing out my precious cargo, Tami and I were in our local supermarket, when she started in on me about my jam again. I had had enough. I turned to her and lectured, "You just don't know what I know, Tami, so you don't understand how special this is. I'm the connoisseur, and you obviously can't appreciate that. When we find something like this, we should treasure it and be thankful we can have it while it lasts. You need to act."

Get over yourself— now—and know what you don't know!

"But you spent lots of money on the jam and hundreds of dollars to ship it across the border . . ." she said.

"Yes, I did!" I interrupted, puffing out my chest with pride. "Because I can, and look at the experience and the joy that brought everyone! You can't get this anywhere else and . . ."

Tami interrupted me with a knowing smirk and pointed behind me: "Are you kidding me? Turn *around.*"

I turned around and there was the Canadian jam—cans of it covering the shelves of our supermarket. For two bucks each.

Just because you don't believe something is possible doesn't mean it isn't true. Just because you don't see something doesn't mean it isn't there. Think about something you do or see the same way many times a year: the way you drive home or the train you take, what you see on your walk around the neighborhood or while you stare out your kitchen or office window. You may be *seeing* as you do these things, but they become so familiar you stop really *looking* and miss something big: When did that building go up? When did the Wilsons paint their house? Has that store been here all along? When did that giant display of my precious Canadian jam appear in my supermarket?

In the same way, it is far too easy to get tunnel vision with a "because I can" attitude, especially when at first we succeed—to get so distracted by the stories we tell in the present that we fail to create new ones for the future. So what if you're a CEO kicking ass or successful entrepreneur whose startup is taking off? So what if you've booked a few speaking gigs and you can charge more? I have been around too many people who, after small and ongoing successes, walk around like that is all that matters: to sustain that success.

> *Thinking big and acting bigger is not about believing that you are big and walking around like you know better. That way lies Jeffy's Jam.*

Losing a sense of awareness is about more than losing perspective. Losing perspective is about failing to stay connected and seeing things from all angles, like when I saw myself in my rugby team photo and realized just how much bigger I was than the other players—something I never saw on the field. I lost perspective about how big I was when I played, but I was never unaware about what I needed to do and what I needed to learn. Losing perspective is about the present as it applies to now. Losing awareness is about the present as it applies to the future. If I had lost awareness, I might have been aware I was big, but I would have stopped working hard to make myself better, not just bigger. I would have quit learning and developing new skills and strengths. I would have given up trying to understand the game at new levels and relied on what I already knew how to do because it was good enough for now.

➤ Losing perspective leaves you unconnected to what is happening *now* and the things you should know to act on.

➤ Losing awareness leaves you oblivious in the present to the things you don't know so you stop looking for them and acting on them for *the future.*

Staying aware is in many ways more complicated than keeping perspective, because it requires us to expand everything we have learned so far, from owning new stories to being thoughtful (if a bit irrational) to listening to our people and customers to steamrolling obstacles. But the consequences are just as dire. Not being in a constant state of awareness of who we are, how we are perceived, the trends in our industries, and how we (and our competitors) are doing things means we aren't thinking beyond what we know.

To do this we need to learn a new dance: We need to stay grounded in the present to focus, connect, and steamroll obstacles and look beyond them to know what we don't know. Learning the steps to this dance starts now.

WHAT IT MEANS TO KNOW WHAT YOU DON'T KNOW

Before you go all Errol Morris vs. Donald Rumsfeld on me, let me tell you something about the former Secretary of Defense's most famous quote. It went like this: "There are known knowns. These are things we know that we know. There are known unknowns. That is to say, there are things that we know we don't know. But there are also unknown unknowns. There are things we don't know we don't know."

No matter how you feel about the former Secretary of Defense, he was right. Without judgment on him or the context of his quote, no one should dismiss his words as pure political gobbledygook, especially businesspeople.

Too many times we think we have gotten our business to where it is supposed to and will always be and stop thinking about what is left to learn in the present, not just the future. In other words, too often we get by just focusing on the known knowns.

Behavioral psychologists will tell you this is a legacy of the way our primitive selves were wired: We focus on what matters to survive now; those are the highest-value targets. Yet, it is the things we know we don't know and don't act on or prepare for *and* the things we don't know we don't know and don't strive to figure out that stop us from thinking big and acting bigger. That's why focus only got you part of the way through this book.

> *When companies get too confident or complacent is when the unknowns really get them.*

Known Unknowns

These are the possibilities you have considered even in a small way and can act or react against. You may not know when they are going to happen or even if they will, but you can prepare for them and be ready if and when they do. This applies to crisis plans for when something big or awful happens, like a recall or an accident that costs lives, as well as little things:

> That someone out there doesn't like your service, product, or you
> That people aren't telling you the whole truth or are lying
> That another company somewhere is doing things differently (or the same for a lower price)
> That changes in technology are coming

Knowing these unknowns leaves you and your people better prepared to anticipate the problems and attack them when they happen. We can and must be aware of, understand, and prepare for these things, even if we don't know *exactly* who is doing them or when or where they are happening. Fail to do that, and you end up like Kodak, which focused exclusively on film even as its people basically invented the digital camera. But at least someone at Kodak knew that digital cameras were a possibility; the company just decided not to act bigger on that innovation and keep innovating in what it knew.

Unknown Unknowns

The unknown unknowns are the things that get us when we focus so much on what we know that we fail to acknowledge there are things we don't even know we don't know. In military terms, think of unknown unknowns like facing rogue commanders. You might prepare for contingencies against commanders who trained the way you did, but rogue commanders don't follow your strategies and rules. They say, "I can play by any rules, because I can!" Moreover, they know what you are going to do because they know the playbook you follow. Heck, they might have even trained with you and know what you know. So they do something totally unexpected that disrupts all your plans for what they *might* do and often succeed despite a David vs. Goliath situation. (For a perfect example of how this played out in a harmless way, check out Malcolm Gladwell's book *Blink* and his discussion of the war games leading up to the Second Gulf War.)

In business today, unknown unknowns are often called disruptive innovations or disruptive technologies. In fact, "innovative" has become synonymous with "disruptive," not just thinking and acting bigger or differently. Think Apple and its Macintosh, Amazon and its digital bookstore, Uber and its taxi app. These companies didn't play by the rules of their competitors and won. Countless others have failed in their wars of disruption, but even though they didn't win the war, they often did damage to their targets' bottom lines and reputations.

The first step to knowing what you don't know: Get over yourself and act bigger.

How does a company respond when these unknowns become known? In other words, what happens when a company sees what is really going on around it and says, "I was not aware of that"? When awareness overtakes complacency, you need to do more than throw a hissy fit and say the competition is just not playing fair (which is essentially what taxi companies did when Uber took off). If there is nothing illegal going on, how do you react to something you never anticipated?

Hubris may be defined as insolence and lead to punishment by the gods of business (your customers and competition). But it is only hubris when you fail because your pride and self-confidence blinded you to what you really needed to do. To understand this on a deeper level, let's consider two companies that had built massive success and faced failure for not being aware of the unknowns: Cadillac and Domino's Pizza.

ADMITTING YOU SUCK

What makes a company admit in the most public way possible that its namesake product sucks? In 2010, Domino's Pizza not only said it in a major advertising campaign, but also showed actual social media posts and focus group footage of their customers saying the pizza tasted "boring," "flavorless," "the worst," and most commonly "like cardboard." Employees at the company headquarters, from the chefs to the PR people to the senior management to CEO Patrick Doyle, also read and responded to customers' comments.

When I saw this commercial for the first time on TV, I was stunned. Who in their right mind would actually do that—spend millions of dollars on a national TV campaign to tell the world your product was awful? How risky was it to go and admit to your customers that you suck? Companies, not just in food, come out with "improved" products all the time, but they never actually say that what the improved product replaced *sucked*. Miracle Whip had run a campaign in which it showed people loving or hating its product, but at least they showed the love. I couldn't remember anyone saying "We are making an inferior product, and we're running advertising to tell you about it!"—and certainly not on the scale of Domino's. Who made that decision, and why?

I went to Ann Arbor to find the answer for my TV show the *C-Suite with Jeffrey Hayzlett* (http://c-suitetv.com/video/why-dominos-spent-millions-to-fix-its-pizza/) and learned the answer was all about awareness: Domino's found out it didn't know what it didn't know.

Domino's may be the world leader in pizza delivery and a large, publicly traded company with annual revenues in excess of $1.5 billion, but it started as small as can be in 1960 as a single pizza shop, Domi-Nick's, in Ypsilanti, Michigan. The company headquarters are in Ann

Arbor, just ten miles from that original location, but the stores are *everywhere*. The company grew like no other fast food franchise in the 1980s, opening more than 4,000 stores. In 2012, it opened its 9,999th store in Carlsbad, California, and days later opened its 10,000th in Istanbul, Turkey, just one of 70 countries around the world in which it operates. In fact, more than half of Domino's sales now come from outside the U.S., and it is the top pizza deliverer in Mexico, the United Kingdom, Australia, India, France, South Korea, and Turkey. The stores around the world combine to deliver more than 1 million pizzas a day worldwide.

Yet, in some ways, Domino's is less one big business than a unified group of small and medium-sized businesses with deep company ties: 95 percent of its stores are franchise-owned, and 90 percent of those franchisees started out by working there. Together, they had been united under one brand promise for more than 50 years: to be the best pizza-delivery company in the world—"best" meaning "fastest," getting your order delivered in 30 minutes or less. Domino's was not about taste; it was about convenience and speed—a promise that dated back to the original Domi-Nick's.

The truth is, Domino's knew this already. It was a known known that its pizza wasn't the best. It cared more about getting us the box than what was *in* the box. And so did we. In college, my friend and I didn't order Domino's every Sunday night and wait for the deliciousness to arrive; we started our watch, hoping that we'd get a pizza for free if it arrived late. Taste did not matter.

That would all change when Domino's said its pizza sucked.

Imagine the risks this involved. You're a food business that has grown exponentially and sold thousands and thousands of franchises to people who for decades have sunk their life savings into your business and brand promise: Give people what they want, fast. Now you realize: You suck. Not you personally or the people who have invested their professional lives in you, but the product that defines the business, and it needs to change. *Has* to change. First, you're telling everyone who thought it was good enough that they are wrong. Second, you are doing away with the very promise that defined what you do.

What if it doesn't work? Is the next thing to come back and say that you suck *more*? Finally, Domino's was certainly doing well enough. Brand recognition was high, and business had been by most measures successful and profitable.

So why take these risks and change when things are good? Why does someone stand up in a meeting and say, "We need to change. This is not working right. We are not good"?

Simply put, Domino's listened beyond the bottom line to the customers who were saying they wanted more and responded. Research showed those customers' palates were changing—what they *valued* was changing. They still wanted a fast delivery, but not at the expense of flavor. Taste and quality mattered. Domino's saw this change as permanent and inevitable and started a race against time to get there. It started remaking and re-baking everything, and when the company was ready it decided to do something really radical: tell the truth. *Domino's owned what they had been and what they had done and communicated it openly, honestly, and transparently. In saying they sucked, they also said, "We listened to you, and we are aware. Our chefs are going to satisfy your taste buds and give you the best quality product for the money."*

This is a lesson in honesty parents give their kids all the time, but those same parents seem to forget these lessons in business, especially when they reach the boardroom. That's because most of the time we are taught that in business, honesty does not pay.

> *Never underestimate the value of honest and open communication and radical transparency to address and find out what you don't know.*

What I learned at Domino's underscores essential lessons in genuine leadership when it comes to finding out what you don't know and thinking big and acting bigger. Take a look at those lessons:

Listen to Your Customers

For years, companies have hidden behind emails that go nowhere, online help that never seems to *be* online, and 800 numbers with endless options ("If you want to talk to a representative . . . good luck."). We have forced customers to comply with our own policies and procedures, but through social media, the voice of the customer has become more critical and provided opportunities for genuine two-way dialogue. Listen to them, and you might find something you don't know that leads to radical change.

Respond to Your Customers

Once you have decided to listen to your customers, you need to make sure you are responding to what they *really* want and know exactly what they are talking about. Domino's had heard the complaints for years about its pizza, but once the company had committed to the change, it made sure it was responding exactly to what the biggest complaints were. Today, it replies regularly to complaints *and* compliments online. Do you?

Listen and Respond to Your People, Too

Even when we are listening to our customers, we are too willing to make decisions without listening to, responding to, and involving our best assets: our people. If you've owned who you are and cleaned your own bathroom, you have a connection top to bottom with your people. *Use it.* Ask them, without consequences, to tell you what they really think, offer ideas to help solve the problem, and have a stake in delivering the results. Domino's showed how it did this in its commercial using real employees to tell the story of what sucked, how they felt about the criticism, and how they helped enact change.

Take a Risk

If something has disrupted your business, you are not going to win by striking back with small, measured steps—"Now with tastier sauce!" That's about thinking small. Remember: No one is going to die. Taking risks can be great if everyone (including you!) who is taking that risk says, "Because we can!"—everyone is aware of where you want to go and is genuinely 100 percent committed top to bottom.

Be "Radical" by Being Transparent, Open, and Honest

Whether it takes a crisis or simply a moment of serious self-scrutiny, the most important thing is that we act honestly when we act radically.

• • •

That last point is the key: Can you engage in real, honest communication? If you are claiming to be authentic, you had better actually be authentic, because someone will find you out.

What if Domino's staged the focus groups? What if it used actors instead of employees in its commercials? What if it wrote those customer complaints itself? How long do you think it would have taken for that to leak and social media to spread it everywhere? Domino's got real instead and used genuine radical transparency. Telling its customers the pizza sucked worked. Domino's sales grew 14.5 percent. As I write this, its stock has doubled to an all-time high. Around the Super Bowl, they would have run out of pepperoni if its executives hadn't gotten in trucks to deliver more to the stores. No word if they made it in 30 minutes or less.

The key for Domino's, and any company that engages in such a dramatic reboot, is to not fall back in the same trap that got it there. Domino's knows the consequences of not maintaining the promises it has made, relationships it has forged, and awareness of what it does not know. It has to: Everyone from microwave brands to chains like Papa John's and Little Caesars to local pizza places and beyond are constantly competing for business. To stay ahead and maintain brand loyalty, Domino's will need to stay active on social media and continue to adapt by listening and innovating with its menu and services. To that end, Domino's is focusing on ordering and delivery again with its app replacing the landline phone and removing the middlemen between the customers and the pizza.

But consider this: What if Domino's had been listening to its customers all along, but instead of finding out that its pizza was figuratively on life support found out that its customers, and thus its brand, were almost literally on life support? This is not an uncommon situation for brands that have lasted a generation or more. Though Domino's was down, it was still dominant when it made its decision to change and be radically transparent about it. How does a company that has been fading regroup and get its mojo back? How do you step back from catastrophic events (from bankruptcy to a bad economy to gains by your competitors to employee problems) or just the brutal advance of Father Time, realize you are not the iconic brand you used to be, and recover?

That's what Cadillac had to do. All the current value of the brand had been transferred to the audience that had bought it for years, and it rode that audience to the edge of the grave. Cadillac still had cachet with collectors, but a vintage sensibility, while great for classic car collectors, does nothing for the current bottom line.

CAN DOWN-AND-OUT COMPANIES GET THEIR MOJO BACK?

Sometimes brands die—even iconic brands. I imagine one of the hardest things to do in shooting period movies from just the past few decades is digitally restoring all the store signs and billboards for brands that have passed away. But what if, like the Man in Black in *The Princess Bride*, you are only "mostly dead"—on life support but still breathing? It doesn't do any good to point fingers, make excuses, or shut the door and pretend things are okay. And there's no Miracle Max out there with a magic chocolate pill to revive you, I assure you. So how does a once-strong company regroup and get its mojo back?

That's the question I wanted answered when I went to Cadillac (http://c-suitetv.com/video/cadillac-c-suite-with-jeffrey-hayzlett/). Cadillac had to overcome "old" perceptions but still retain its brand distinctiveness. Sure, it never went away. The brand has always meant something—but what and to whom? The luxury vehicle division of General Motors, Cadillac was founded in Detroit in 1902, and by the 1950s it was synonymous with "best" and "coolest." But by the 21st century, anyone under 40 thought the Cadillac brand was for old people. Calling something "The Cadillac of . . ." was neither meaningful to a new generation of consumers, nor necessarily a compliment. "The Mercedes of" something—that meant the best. That's the brand that has been doing really, really well with the car buyers Cadillac wanted back: Mercedes, followed by BMW and Lexus.

"Hey, Cadillac, it's Oldsmobile calling. I've got a seat on the bus to oblivion waiting for you. . . ."

Then came bankruptcy and a bad economy, and Cadillac finally realized it was far from the iconic brand it used to be. To come back from catastrophic events like these, overcome old perceptions, and still retain its distinctiveness, Cadillac needed to ask two questions: What the hell are we doing, and why are we doing it that way?

Discussions like this are the most important ones leaders can have. Whether things are good or desperate, you must figure out the core of what your company stands for and do what needs to be done to get back to that core. Yes, sometimes it's that simple. Don't believe me? Can *you* answer this question? *What unknowns exist inside the "walls" of your company?* Sure, all businesses have different cadences, products, services, and people. But every business has a mirror they can look in, and the bigger the better. Cadillac told me they had these "mirror moments" by asking another really tough question: *How did we get so far away from what we were? The answer: Cadillac lost touch with what the people they needed actually wanted.*

Cadillac *thought* they were doing this all along. They made adjustments to some of the trends and features of other luxury carmakers. But that amounted to course correcting in a fishbowl. Small thinking never leads to big changes, but Cadillac didn't know what big thinking and actions to take. It couldn't say what a mid-30s professional wanted in a car that screamed luxury, quality, power, and success. How could it expect to when people see it as what old people drive—low and slow?

Cadillac realized much later than Domino's, with its promise of delivery time over taste, that it was in touch with relics of a bygone era—a bankrupt company in a bankrupt city. It needed to be a phoenix from the ashes, and that meant radical change. Realizing the company had no idea what the customers it needed wanted, it stopped making small changes that addressed what it thought people wanted and actually talked to those people. It brought in people like them to work at the company and made sure everyone in the company felt great about the brand by sharing the direction it was taking. *It became aware of what it didn't know and developed a plan for serving a younger audience by getting back to that core of being the best and most desired.*

Today, Cadillac has moved past Lexus into the third position, with only BMW and Mercedes to beat. I may not be young, but I'm not old, and I have been impressed in a way I never was before about the brand. That's a start. But day in and day out, Cadillac must continually ask how to make the brand bigger and sexier—and attack those unknowns. Its leaders must not simply say, "Now we are listening." They must ask, "What makes us think we are listening now?"

A company of any size that is facing a situation like Cadillac's—which can happen after a few years as easily as it happens after a hundred— understands these essential lessons for dealing with unknowns and acting bigger in the right ways to help jumpstart your business from the inside out.

Shift the Mood

Everyone I met at Cadillac, from the assembly line to the C-Suite, was really excited about the brand. You could *feel* the mood shifting. They had a "Hey, we're back. This is what's happening, and it's exciting" attitude. This goes beyond cadence and is connected to mood. It was an awareness of what they once were, but a determination *not* to be the *brand* they once were—to be a brand with the same stature in a newer, more relevant way with a new audience.

Avoid Course Correcting into Oblivion

It doesn't matter how good you are, you *can* course correct into oblivion. You have to step back and realize you don't know where you are or where you're going. You don't need a catastrophic event like bankruptcy, a bad economy, or the realization that you're not the iconic brand you used to be to do this. You just have to ask, "What the hell are we doing, and why are we doing it that way?" Cadillac kept changing and altering its cars in little ways to the point where they looked like amalgams of various makes and models. No one knew what it was anymore—it had no identity to anyone except those who remembered what it used to be.

Work to Overcome Perceptions and Expand Your Audience

In marriage, it's nice to grow old together. Not in business. Cadillac had an audience it literally rode to death, meaning it depended on the same customers—our fathers and grandfathers—who continued to buy Cadillac until they died. Cadillac is in the process of reinventing and redesigning the brand to attract that younger audience, but it must do this *continually* to show it is committed to those customers. If that means it might alienate some of its existing loyal older customers? Well, those customers weren't going to be driving for much longer anyway!

"THE TRUTH IS OUT THERE"

I could have chosen any number of companies large and small instead of Cadillac and Domino's as examples in this chapter. But that's the point: Their stories are familiar. And I also know it makes me sound a little like a dad to quote the opening line from a 1990s TV show for this section, but hey, *The X-Files* is coming back to TV and a whole new generation will learn the show is dead-on: The truth is out there, so look for it.

That's what awareness is leading to: a truer sense of who and where you are—not absolute truth, not perfection, not a permanent condition, just a sense of what opportunities are there, what's coming that you may not see, and what's possible.

> *The longer you have been successful doing what you do, the more you have to work to avoid tunnel vision.*

We've all done this before. Remember what I said about your morning commute on the same route home every day? How often do you look at what's new around you as you go? Pay attention: *Look* out the window and be aware! Stop right now and ask yourself these questions:

- ➤ What are the key attributes of your business, according to you? What do your employees and customers say? Are they saying the same things you are?
- ➤ What do you suck at, and what don't you know? What do your employees and customers say? Are they saying the same things you are?

I am always, *always*, looking at how my businesses do things and what is going on around them: What are the trends and the things I don't know? That's why I can play and survive in a young man's game like digital marketing. The simplest way for a business to start doing this is to be a customer of your business. I've done this for decades to stay ahead. When my B2B label company sold out to a bigger conglomerate that everyone said had great sales and customer service, I didn't just take their word—I went to work. I took some of the orders and spoke to the customers. I placed orders for customers and made people I knew place orders and report back. Not surprisingly, the stories I heard about the company did not match reality: The biggest threat was *not* the competition but how we treated our customers.

We all know awareness of others and who we are helps us in our personal and professional lives, so why not in our business? When you start a new job or relationship, you're hyper-aware of your boss's or partner's needs. You're attentive to every detail—it's new and you're excited. Then the flowers stop coming. You stop answering emails or returning calls right away, you cut people off more as they speak, or you just stop listening. Things are good enough, so you let yourself go. You don't ask questions like: What can I do better now? What can I do better next time? How can I improve? How much better can it be?

It's easy to ask these questions when things are desperate. But how much did you ask them when things were going well? When was the last time you asked them after you kicked ass? Did you even ask them at all?

As I said at the beginning, businesses and people fall into powerful stories that make us act big, small, or not at all. These stories are how we understand the world today, and we use them to create the realities we want to believe. Stop believing the stories that you've been telling and start writing new ones, especially if you are in your prime. I guarantee you that the greatest athletes practice harder than anyone else. The winners are on the field first and off it last. They study and adapt to highlight their strengths and overcome or transcend their weaknesses and beat the competition. Businesses, like athletes, that get too locked down in who they are fall victim to hubris—all because they focus on who they are, not on what they don't know.

And if all that did not make this lesson sink in, then let me leave you with a story about a speech I gave Down Under and how easy it is, even if you have been successful in the past, to fail to do the work you need to do to avoid tunnel vision. My family had travelled with me to Australia for my talk, and I worked into my speech how we had done all the touristy things the previous day and how wonderfully exhausting it was, especially for my wife, Tami. I told the audience something like: "Tami had the fanny pack, and I kept going in and out of it with the camera all day. All day long I'm grabbing her fanny pack and taking pictures. I'm in and out and in and out of that thing all day taking pictures."

The audience laughed hysterically, and I thought, "I'm killing it! Damn, I'm good." I knew I had them. *I knew it.*

After the speech, someone came up to me and thanked me for my presentation but wondered if I knew that *fanny* has a different meaning in Australia than the United States?

"What? Fanny packs are things you wear on your bum, right?"

"Yes, but the fanny in Australia is slang for, um . . ." he leaned over and whispered, "a woman's *vagina*. And to pack a fanny . . ."

So I was telling the audience I was in and out and in and out all day long. . . . Oh, my.

Then I thought, "That's awesome!" And I don't mean sarcastically. Since no one died, I wasn't going to worry about it—just laugh. I had learned from my mistake with my cans of "rare" Canadian blueberry jam just how easily one can go from losing perspective to losing awareness, and this was an innocent, if racy, reminder never to forget that lesson.

It was also a stark reminder that no matter how hard you try, you can't and won't know everything. But what matters is how *prepared* you are to handle it. Keep looking for truths—the known unknowns and unknown unknowns. Never forget there are always things that you don't even know you don't know, and let the desire to learn them drive you to think big and act bigger even if you are at the top of your game. This is what awareness leads to: a truer ongoing sense of where you are now and where you might go in the future. Not absolutely, not perfectly, just genuinely and selflessly by getting over yourself—*now*—

and knowing what you don't know! Stop walking around like you know better and be aware. Along the other way lie filled cases of overpriced jam, inappropriate talk about having sex with your wife in front of a foreign audience, and worse. Being aware lets you see what is possible as you push your big thinking to ask, "What's next?"

LESSONS LEARNED: KNOW WHAT YOU DON'T KNOW

I cannot repeat this enough: Get over yourself—*now*—and know what you don't know:

> *Avoid tunnel vision*: Losing perspective leaves you unconnected in the present; losing awareness leaves you oblivious in the present.

> *Don't get too confident or complacent*: Know your unknowns.

> *Never underestimate the value of honest and open communication and radical transparency*: Listen to your customers, respond to your customers and your people, and take risks.

> *Ask*: What the hell are we doing, and why are we doing it that way? Then shift the mood, avoid course correcting into oblivion, and continually work to overcome perceptions and expand your audience.

The best way to do any of this is to constantly ask questions of yourself and others that force more than yes/no answers: What are the trends and the things I don't know? What are the key attributes of my business? What do my employees and customers say they are? Are they saying the same things I am? What do I suck at, and what don't I know? What do my employees and customers say? Are they saying the same things I am? Just like great athletes and their coaches, business leaders can use these questions to stay aware and adapt to highlight their strengths, overcome or transcend their weaknesses, and beat the competition.

CHAPTER NINE

FIND a BIGGER POND

Always Ask, "What's Next?"

W hen I was CMO of Kodak, I thought I was a big deal doing $17 billion a year in sales—a bigger number than anything I had remotely been responsible for before. Then I found myself talking with Dan Henson, then the CMO of General Electric, who told me GE needed to *grow* by $15 billion a year just to meet its expected sales targets. That's when I realized a fundamental truth in thinking big and acting bigger: No matter how big you think you are, there is always somebody bigger.

Consider the case of Henry Ford. Ford's innovations, entrepreneurial spirit, and ability to overcome his initial failures to create the assembly line that led to the rise of the automobile is a familiar story. But did you know

> *There is* always *somebody* bigger.

Henry Ford designed his Model T to run on gasoline *and* ethanol? For the 20 years it was produced, the Model T was a "flex fuel" car. With a flip of a switch, it could go from ethanol to gas and back.

You see, Ford was a pragmatist (he famously used the crates his cars' parts came in as floorboards). He wanted his cars to be affordable and practical for the common man, but in 1908 (the first year the Model T was produced), there could be hundreds of miles before a driver saw a sign for gas to fill the car's ten-gallon tank. What they did see by the side of the road were farms filled with corn, which could be used to produce plenty of gallons of another fuel: ethanol. Ethanol was already gaining notice in the scientific community for its cleaner burning and better mileage, and Ford saw it as valuable to the future of cars, even if just to give drivers more fueling options. Ford had every intention of making ethanol at least as much of an option as gasoline. He even invested in that future, building the largest ethanol plant in the country at the time.

So what happened? Why is this story mostly lost to history? Someone bigger got in Ford's way: namely John D. Rockefeller. Even after the U.S. Supreme Court broke up Rockefeller's Standard Oil Trust as an illegal monopoly in 1911, Rockefeller and the companies that Standard Oil became fought for more than a decade to eliminate the competition of ethanol. Of course, Rockefeller did not want to eliminate *Ford*. That would be the business definition of cutting off your nose to spite your face. Ford's massively successful cars ran on gasoline, too. Rockefeller simply wanted ethanol out of the equation.

Ford, however, proved to be a resilient foe. Rockefeller finally won only with a full-throated support of Prohibition, which banned the production of *any* alcohol in America. Ford didn't have a chance. He continued making flex fuel Model Ts until the car ceased production in 1927, but that was still years before Prohibition ended in 1933. Rockefeller's win was so definitive that no commercially available car in the world ran on ethanol again for a half-century.

In the end, Henry Ford thought big and acted bigger, but even though he was among the biggest businessmen in America, he lost his fuel battle to Rockefeller. There is always a chance that will happen when might meets might. But no one accuses Henry Ford of playing small ball. He was willing to do what we all must do to keep winning: Ask, "What's next?"

> *If you've been fearless, bold, and relentless in thinking and acting bigger to this point, it's time to think about moving on or up in everything you do and ask, "What's next?"*

WHAT'S NEXT: FIND A BIGGER POND

It doesn't matter how relentless you've been or how innovative you are. It doesn't matter whether you've been in business for days or decades, or how many millions or billions you have in revenue. You must keep driving forward. Even if you want to stay the size you are and be a purpose-driven company, your purpose isn't going to have much promise if your competitors start filling the space around your pond. Even if you *are* at the top, someone or something is gaining on you or sees you as a threat and is trying to take you out.

To keep things going and going after the things you want, you must find a bigger pond, make new ponds, expand and stretch the pond you're "fishing" in, or maybe move to new water bodies and go deep-sea fishing.

To begin your search for a bigger pond, ask yourself:

- ➤ What's next?
- ➤ What do we need to do to reach our bigger goals?
- ➤ How will our brand, services, products, technologies, and above all our people keep standing out from the rest?

Companies ignore or pay lip service to the second question at their peril, especially when it comes to people. While size does matter, people matter more. Size is just about scale. The more people who are driven around the focus of where a company wants to go, the more it moves in that direction. Remember: There is *always* someone bigger. The real

> *Size matters,*
> *but people*
> *matter more.*

secret is what gets your heart beating, and you need to stay heart-healthy for the workout ahead.

That's what I have done. I made myself big in Sioux Falls and then found a bigger pond on the state level. When I was big in South Dakota, I realized there are 49 other states out there to get bigger in. I can do it in Iowa. I can do it nationwide. I can do it in North America, Latin America, Europe, and around the world. And once I go global, there are *spaceships.*

OK, the spaceships are still a few years away, but when we get there, I will do what I have always done to seize the opportunity: scale myself, stretch, find balance, and then reinvent and adapt again, all the while making sure I always stay true to who I am. *That's the real balance in this chapter: between shifting your business to something else and not leaving your identity behind. You can create bigger and badder stories to tell, but authenticity is paramount no matter how big you get.*

That said, authenticity cannot stop time: You can't get stuck watching your customers die like Cadillac or being a big fish in an ever-dwindling pond like Kodak with film. Just because you are innovative now doesn't mean you will still be innovative next year. It is not enough to know the unknown; you need to have the courage to act in that unknown space. You need to keep refining and innovating: to go beyond where you are, explore what is emerging, and act—even if that means blowing up everything you know before the pond runs dry.

I always think about reality-TV king Mark Burnett. He was a sergeant in the British Army in the Falklands before he made his way into infomercials. When infomercials peaked, he found a bigger reality pond that led to successful shows like *Survivor, Shark Tank,* and *The Voice.* Mark is British, and I'm not sure what the cricket equivalent is of hitting a home run, but that is what he did: hit a home run and then, like all sluggers, started over when he came to bat again. And what a good hitter always knows is that it only gets harder to get hits as the game and season go on; you must continually work to stay ahead of the pitchers and the other teams.

The key is never being satisfied with the way things are. That way lies mediocrity. You have to be willing to start over—to go back to the beginning, taking all you have learned and applying it to what's next. Find that new and bigger pond. To do so successfully, you must at the very least be willing to do three things:

1. Adapt
2. Ask
3. Automate

Should the time come when that isn't enough, you must then be willing to think about selling what you have to get what you want. But if you do, don't forget that other essential "A": Authenticity.

RE-ENVISION THE POND: ADAPT

As I said in Chapter 2, people scoffed when, after I got my own prime-time show on Bloomberg, I pulled it and took it in-house as part of my own C-Suite Network (http://c-suitetv.com/) and the business channel on United Airlines. People come up with all kinds of reasons why I did it. A lot of them think it had to have been cancelled because it was not successful. That's pure hate fiction. It was the top prime-time business show on TV. The first shows totaled 5.1 million impressions on Twitter and reached roughly 15 million Facebook accounts. In fact, the reason I took it in-house was *because* it was so successful. I knew something bigger was out there *and* remembered my golden rule of adaptation:

> *The speed of business today makes adaptation more essential than ever. You must strike a balance between satisfying demand for who you are and what you offer now and adapting.*

In the case of my show, I loved being on Bloomberg, but it was more about fit for the future. I also had my own network and a preponderance of evidence that TV is being produced and consumed differently than ever

If you want to be bigger, you need to adapt or change proactively while you are successful.

before. Consumers expect to be able to watch what they want, when they want, how they want, where they want, and as much as they want at a time. I did not have that kind of control over my show, and now I do.

You can always tell the companies that have found balance from the ones that haven't, because they usually spin off the business that successfully found the bigger pond or sold the one that got left behind in the old one. Think eBay and PayPal, 21st Century Fox and News Corp, IBM and Lenovo, and GE and its appliances. Coke bought a piece of Monster Beverages and then gave Monster its energy drinks and took Monster's soda properties to better focus on what each company does best. Fail to make moves like this, and you end up like Radio Shack, on the dust heap of dead electronics brands like Circuit City and CompUSA.

Is there always a bigger pond? No. Electronics chain stores may be retail dinosaurs. But other industries have managed to adapt and thrive despite constant prognostications of their deaths. Take something close to my heart: print.

A generation ago, no one could conceive of a world without print even if they were trying to go "Back to the Future." October 21, 2015, a date that will arrive shortly after the publication of this book, is a landmark day for fans of that film series. That was the day Marty McFly, Doc Brown, and Jennifer Parker visited their future selves in *Back to the Future Part II*. The film came out in 1989, and its creators imagined many fantastical things for the characters to see in 2015: a self-drying, auto-fitting jacket, robotic dog walkers, hover skateboards, and cars that need no roads. To their credit, they also got some things right, including video conferencing, which is what future adult Marty is doing with a colleague when their boss catches them conspiring to do something they shouldn't.

"You are terminated!" screams his boss. "Read my fax!"

Suddenly, fax machines all over the McFly house spit out pages saying, "You're fired." Apparently, filmmakers in 1989 could imagine a world where video replaced phones but not print. Neither can we in the real 2015. While fax machines are on the verge of extinction, many in the print industry have survived by changing what they do—but not who they are.

When Don Lowe, the CEO of Franchise Services, Inc., which owns the brands Sir Speedy and PIP, started franchising in the 1960s, stores were mom and pop businesses. Dad did the printing and Mom worked the front counter; customer walked in, placed an order with Mom, and Dad went to work printing. When Don's son Richard joined the company, the same year *Back to the Future Part II* hit theaters, it was the same way. Today, all that has changed.

"When I started 25 years ago," Richard says, "about a third of our business was business cards, letterhead, envelopes, and forms, and the walk-in customer came from a two-mile radius. We were a manufacturing business with a narrow product line. Today, customers come from anywhere, coast-to-coast, due to our e-commerce capabilities, and, although we are still a manufacturing business, our product line is more diverse, covering everything from printed products to signage and integrated marketing campaigns for our clients."

Print businesses used to be highly commoditized: low cost and repeatable. Today, those businesses have moved in the opposite direction: 67 percent of Franchise Services' business is customized marketing collateral. As Don notes, "What we provide today is not commoditized in any way. The majority of our work is based on the customers' needs. We collaborate with them to understand their objectives and develop a solution that may or may not be just a printed document. For example, if a company is launching a product, it could start with a single direct-mail piece but be combined with a new targeted mailing list, the design of a website and brochure, and even signage and social media integration. It has changed so dramatically, but the value has gone much higher."

To add this value in any business, especially one that franchises, means more than adapting at the top. If you adapt but your people or customers who have been with you for a long time do not (or fail to understand the changes), your business falls out of alignment.

Adapt at the speed that businesses communicate, but make sure your team and your customers are still running beside you as you do.

As Don notes, "One of the challenges some of our franchisees face is changing from where they have been for the last 30 years to where they need to be based on where the marketplace is today. We are no longer the retail shop that prints ink on paper. Technology in our business has changed by providing us with the capability to meet the changing needs of our clients such as more customization and one-to-one marketing."

Interestingly, adapting in the print world has had the benefit of making it attractive to younger generations, who see opportunity and excitement in customization over commoditization. According to the Lowes, a decade ago no son or daughter wanted to take over his or her parents' printing business, slogging away with one-off drudgery. They are coming back to the business now that the business offers more than print, such as print integrated with the internet, apps, and social media. "They are finding it exciting and different than they thought it was," says Richard. "It doesn't have the moniker of 'we are a printing company' around it anymore."

The reason? These businesses *aren't* printing companies. They are visual communications businesses producing collateral marketing that needs to stand out. They are selling communication and connection. To do that, they need to adapt at the speed that businesses communicate.

Just ask Jaycen Thorgeirson, founder and CEO of UviaUs, whose young company was attracted to print and visual communication. At first, the company focused on unique direct marketing print material for organizations like the Washington Nationals baseball team. Then, in 2011, Jaycen saw a tool for embedding video technology in marketing being used in Europe and started investigating it. Today, UviaUs is 100 percent focused on its Uvideo as a dynamic marketing tool that fuses audio, video, and print.

What's interesting is that UviaUs got more resistance internally than externally for this change, which was also the case with Franchise Services, and reinforces the importance of adapting with your people in alignment. In the case of UviaUs, the salespeople faced price resistance: Uvideo was much more expensive compared to the traditional print media customers were doing. But the company pushed forward without excuses. Sure, it required a higher investment, but they also attracted a higher level of clientele that saw the value in the delivery method and its adaptability for more targeted marketing.

In the end, UviaUs found the brands it worked with *expected* the company to do something different to help them stand out. What mattered most to UviaUs and its customers was not the product but delivering on the promise of what they sold. Products must change; the goals for those products do not. "We are still you-via-us. This is still printed collateral and marketing," says Jaycen. "This is about brand experience, and our customers get how valuable it is. They have come to expect that we are going to do something different. They do not want to be a one-trick pony, and neither do we. Otherwise we are not differentiating ourselves."

UviaUs is working hard to expand the bigger pond it is in now. It is helping its partners find new uses and measurement tools to demonstrate ongoing value for its Uvideo so that customers can keep justifying the investment. When Jaycen and his team heard customers ask, "How am I going to use this? Who is going to fulfill it?" UviaUs developed an ecosystem for customers to tap into. The company can help with strategy, content, industrial design, graphic design, video production and service, online integration, technical support—anything a customer needs and wants. It also lowered its barriers to entry and made it easier for new customers to get their feet wet with smaller investments.

UviaUs knew to do this because it did one thing: It *asked* its customers questions and then *listened* to the answers.

FIND NEW PONDS: ASK DIRECTIONS—AND LISTEN TO THE ANSWERS

Expanding your existing customer base through building new stores, acquiring compatible businesses, or tapping new markets or market segments is the classic way to find bigger ponds. Overexpansion is the biggest concern here. Whether because of bad planning, confusion between localized success and broader appeal, caving to shareholder demands for growth, or the lack of capital or people to fund and oversee the expansion, the pitfalls of overexpansion are well documented. Case studies from Krispy Kreme to Pets.com are legendary.

> *Take the time to understand and listen to what your current and potential future customers are telling you before tapping them.*

But there is one rule that when violated will inevitably result in failure or delays, no matter how well you plan or how much capital you have: Your value proposition or the value you think you offer may not translate to new and different markets, whether those markets are demographic, geographic, ethnographic, global . . .

I can't begin to cover in this book the work being done in all the industries to know their customers in various markets. But Glenn Llopis of the Glenn Llopis Group, a Cuban-American entrepreneur, author, speaker, and consultant to Fortune 500 companies, taught my C-Suite Network what happens when you fail to communicate with a market, using the market he knows, works with, and lives in every day as an example: Hispanics.

According to Glenn, what most companies try to do equates to forced assimilation rather than recognizing that Hispanics are a unique market segment defined by their rich culture. As a result, the words we use successfully to reach other markets don't work to drive behavior in the Hispanic market, because those words don't adequately tap into what Hispanics value.

> *We have to value a market enough to appreciate, understand, and respond to it uniquely—not with a one-size-fits-all approach.*

In other words, total or whole market strategies fall completely flat. They can also come across as inauthentic. After all, how are you actually differentiating the target audience from the total market approach if all you do is swap in the "Garcia Family" for the "O'Brien Family" in the same new car ad? You think that reads as genuine to Hispanics? It looks inclusive and in some senses it is—at least the ad people realized not all markets look the same. But photo editing people is a superficial approach at best.

"Here's what people like me think when we see that: Are you just trying to cut costs because you don't care to explore the required intellectual capital requirements to best engage with Hispanics and what our community represents to you? Recognizing the distinction between what the Garcia family looks like and what makes them special is what needs to be understood to connect with them or any immigrant and underserved community. We need to recognize the role Hispanics play as they become the face of America, understand their family values, and capture them in a genuine way to elevate and strengthen our value proposition to them," says Glenn. Yet companies are at a loss to do it any other way than the old way, rather than embrace new ways of thinking. "Historically," he adds, "brands will tell you that they have tried to target Hispanics, and it hasn't been successful because it is very difficult to measure sustainable ROI. I understand that, because that is my mentality, too. But it is a different time now. It is not about history or guessing but establishing a competitive advantage by allowing cultural intelligence to be a strategy for growth."

Glenn suggests we start our approach with one word: "listen"—both to the customers *and* our people who are like those customers. Too often, we don't. Glenn gives a remarkable example from inside the financial services industry—an industry that realizes they have an immediate need and opportunity to tap the Hispanic market—of how much we do not do this. According to his research, $53 billion is attributed to unbanked Latino households, and only 33 percent of high-net-worth Hispanic individuals have retirement plans. Knowing this, a financial services company invited Glenn to present to one of its large annual meetings. Afterward, he met a Colombian couple who worked as representatives at the company. As he listened to their story, Glenn thought, "If I was this company I would train all of my leaders to understand their mindset, because Hispanics are going to fuel my immediate growth needs and represent the future of my clientele. *Every* leader can learn from this couple and recognize how best to serve this underserved community by recognizing what's important to them. Yet nobody was doing that."

Later that evening, when Glenn ran into one of the company's executives, he told him, "I want to introduce you to two of your representatives, but if I do, there are some ground rules: First, I just want you to listen. Thank them for being part of the organization, and ask them, 'What can I do to help?' Second, I want you to stay for at least 15 minutes and *really* pay attention to do that. And then three, tomorrow you have got to send them an email and let them know you appreciate the time that you spent with them." The executive agreed, and Glenn made the introduction and left. "That executive told me he would have never known that potential existed at the company and the market unless I 'discovered' it for him. But I didn't discover anything. I just listened and understood what his people, like so many people like me, need that is different than others. Think about how often it doesn't happen."

It doesn't happen partially because, as we learned in the previous chapter, we think we know what we know and fail to listen to our customers as a proactive rule, not as a reaction. Swap the word Millennial or African-American for Hispanic, and you begin to get the picture. When you ask the right questions and listen to the answers—really *listen*—customers and potential customers will help you understand what you need to do to reach them.

> How have you listened to the market you want to attract?

Consider what Eddie Rausch, the founder of Veteran Tickets Foundation, or Vet Tix, told me. Vet Tix provides family members of troops killed in action, active military, and veterans with free tickets to sporting events, concerts, performing arts, and family activities. The cause is close to my heart, and one would think it was a no-brainer for success. And yet Eddie told me that there was a surprising obstacle to making the pond bigger soon after he launched in 2008—and it didn't come from the supply side. Initially, the families, active military, and veterans were skeptical of the service, thinking it was a little too good to be true. Once they had experienced the service, however, word of mouth spread quickly. But after some growth, suddenly they weren't getting enough customers for the tickets they had.

Eddie wasn't sure why, so he asked his customers. The answer? "We had reached the point that veterans who used the service didn't *want* other veterans to know about the service because they saw them as competition," says Eddie.

The solution? "To solve that problem, we instituted a lottery for great tickets and prizes. Each veteran gets a unique URL or QC Code they can send out to their buddies, and once those buddies sign up and get verified, the veteran gets virtual participation appreciation coins in his or her account. They can use each coin as a chip in the hat for any lottery. So for every buddy you sign up it increases your odds."

Vet Tix grew quickly again after that. They've got a great "veteran wall" and are now working on getting more partners to make the service even better for the people who serve our country.

MOVE FASTER IN YOUR POND: AUTOMATE AND SYSTEMATIZE

Along the way, Eddie also had to find a way to update the company's system to handle a large volume of electronic tickets to eliminate postage and man-hours. That's similar to the problem Jermaine Griggs faced when his business, Hear and Play Music, took off. What he did provides another important lesson in building bigger ponds.

Back to systems again, Jeff? Yes, I am.

If you don't have the resources or manpower to find a bigger pond, you must do the work to make your business faster and better with communication, automation, and systematization so that you find the time to do it.

I love Jermaine Griggs' story. He grew up in his grandmother's one-bedroom apartment with his mom and sister, envisioning life on the other side of the tracks. He found it through music, specifically the songs he spent hours learning to play by ear on the piano his grandmother won on *The Price Is Right*. By the time he was 16, Jermaine was teaching other people in the neighborhood how to play his way. At 17, he used $70 he saved to buy the domain HearandPlay.com and launched Hear and Play Music, an instructional music company specializing in teaching piano by ear.

Flash forward a decade, and HearandPlay.com is now an international "hub" where more than 2 million aspiring musicians download Jermaine's online lessons every year and 300,000 loyal students receive his newsletters. The company has grossed more than $10 million with no funding, no credit, no investors, and one secret weapon: automation. While studying law & criminology at University of California, Irvine, Jermaine relied heavily on automated follow-up and marketing processes to run his business while he made good on a promise to his family to graduate college. What resulted was a unique automation strategy and philosophy that he used to build a thriving business.

"Automation levels that used to be achievable only by big companies with huge numbers of customers and shopping data, giant technological infrastructures, and expensive integrated systems that talk to each other are now affordable and possible at the entrepreneurial level," says Jermaine. "Guys like me with a couple of employees can do things like an Amazon or Microsoft and make those processes generate massive prosperity in our businesses. I can mimic what the big companies do—and do it better—while I play with my kids in my dream home in my pajamas."

That's right, Jermaine is a "pajamapreneur." And as you read this book, someone somewhere in the world is reading a personal email from Jermaine, receiving a weekly text message or tip, getting a birthday card or 30-day "thank you" letter in the mail, every one

> *Words like "automated" and "system" don't contradict the word "personal."*

of them thinking he is thinking about them because he is—just not in the way most people and businesses do. First, Jermaine smartly focused on customer needs and desires, not simply products, and then he did almost all communication through automation. In fact, he has gotten so good at automation, he now teaches it at his new website, http://automationclinic.com.

You can't be so fixated on attracting new customers that you ignore your most valuable asset: happy existing customers who are responsible for most of your profits. But you can't be so fixated on existing customers that you have no time to attract new ones. Simply put, what Jermaine's success shows is if you invest the time and resources like his company does to collect data up front and keep collecting that data through a refined system to really get to know your customers, automation can be exceptionally personal—and personable—and take almost no time when functioning well.

Hear and Play has more than 150 auto-response possibilities based on what a customer clicks, shows interest in, or buys. With every click or purchase tagged, the profile for that customer is further refined and a new set of communications is set for their future, based on their actions and interactions with the company. It has gotten so dynamic even Jermaine cannot predict the path it will go down or what emails a given customer will get, because his automated system is listening and responding as *him*. His customer relationship management is like a doctor's file filled with your entire medical history—available to consult during your next visit and better communicate with you because it looks at that data and talks to *you* based on what is in that file.

"Because I paid attention to my customers' individual needs and actions from the beginning, they don't mind and often never think of my emails and texts as automated," Jermaine says. "I attribute almost all my phenomenal success to the relationships I have with my customers, every bit of which is fueled and strengthened by automated follow-up that comes directly from me—messages and information specifically tailored to them, their interests, behaviors, and needs. They feel personal, not robotic, and even though the correspondence customers get is computer-generated, these systems have grown my bottom line and lifetime customer value by double- and triple-digit percentages!"

How can you get started? Here's some advice I adapted from Jermaine:

- *Stop personally doing anything that's reactive.* Stay in the mode of proactive.
- *Automate any repetitive tasks immediately.* If you have got to say it twice the same way, then make it a system, automate it, and leverage it.

> → *Outsource anything anyone can do as well or better.* Cost, space, and proximity are no longer excuses for not finding help—the world is overflowing with highly qualified vendors.

This last reason is why when I reach points in my business where I could scale back and make more money by focusing on core products, I turn that piece of business over to my team to run while I try to have a bigger impact and discover new ponds. That's fun for me! Still, while automation and great systems can get you far, you still might need help to get to that bigger pond.

COMBINE PONDS: SELL UP, NOT OUT

I spoke to the National Speakers Association in Miami, and afterward the host thanked me for being willing to come to them despite my "meteoric rise in speaking." I was thinking, "Meteoric? I've been doing this for more than 15 years." As I listened, I found myself thinking back over those years, and how many times in speaking and in business I thought, "I'm the top dog!" only to realize, "Holy crap! There's an entirely new level." Every. Time.

Sometimes I reached that next level by adapting. Other times, I needed to combine my strengths with another company like Kodak. I have even acquired companies to make my pond bigger. I have yet to be acquired, but if that time comes, it won't be for money. I know Silicon Valley and the broader tech world build businesses designed to sell to a Facebook or a Google. That is not about ownership, but money—a quick return on investment of time and venture capital. I'm not about that, and neither is this book. I invest everything I am in what I do.

If you care about what you do, merging or selling your business to someone else must still be about you.

If I sold something I owned, and me along with it, it would be to make myself bigger, better, and faster, not just richer. What's next must be about more than money.

That's what Elisa Camahort Page, Jory Des Jardins, and Lisa Stone, the three women who founded and run BlogHer, did. BlogHer is the internet's leading guide to the hottest news and trends among women in social media. In 2005, the three women united around the idea of finding women who blog, bringing them together, and having them engage with their audiences and customers in new ways. These women were involved in blogging when blogging wasn't cool, and they quickly owned the space for women. BlogHer became a zeitgeist that is hard to really fathom in an age when blogging is commonplace. Their initial invitation attracted 300 women who were active online and willing to meet up in person. From there, they built a company and a successful brand with an audience of 100 million across premium blogs, websites, Pinterest, Facebook, and Twitter that aims to educate, empower, and bring more exposure to women writers.

Some might find what BlogHer does limiting over the course of a decade, but not Elisa, Jory, and Lisa. They kept growing and adapting, learning as they went as everything changed rapidly around them. It wasn't easy. As Lisa notes, "The advertising and publishing models we are working with have revolutionized over the past ten years. There has been absolutely shocking acceleration and change in publishing models and that's been an obsession. That is what is harder: It is *much* more complicated and nuanced. Thank God we were an agile startup built in open source software that didn't code ourselves into a corner. Being on the cutting edge of publishing means you are challenged by traditional and cutting-edge media all the time. The community and the sponsors come at us with the smartest questions from the smartest advertisers in the world for the past ten years."

The biggest question: "How do we reach exactly the person we want to reach?"

"We said we can approximate, but that's tough," answers Jory. "We were ahead of the game in terms of approximating. Yet even we had to learn about the targeting technology and how to integrate it. And for BlogHer to get that across to publishers even when we don't necessarily understand it? That has been our challenge. The advertising industry has been shifting to smarter, data-based models, which has choked a lot of traditional media companies. BlogHer has been able to shift, and everything we do has a tech component."

Like my speaking career, some might call BlogHer's success "meteoric." They are a brand name with a thriving network that extends way beyond the internet to its series of branded conferences. But it wasn't meteoric. BlogHer has been doing this for a decade, continually adapting and communicating those changes to its employees and its two sets of customers: the blogging community and its sponsors.

It's the same great story we have heard from the best companies we've discussed in this book: *a story of scaling the right way and making sure that everyone is in alignment around the mission as things change and adapt.*

Only the BlogHer story has a different ending—one that was still being written when I last spoke to them (http://c-suitetv.com/video/executive-perspectives-blogher/). In 2014, when Elisa, Jory, and Lisa found they had done all they could with the resources they had, they decided to sell their company to SheKnows Media, the leading women's lifestyle media company online. BlogHer wants to be faster and bigger and expand globally, and SheKnows provided them with the capital to do that. I have no doubt they will. Maybe after they conquer the world, I'll sit next to them on one of those spaceships as we boldly go where no one has gone before.

I am also sure the reason BlogHer chose SheKnows as a partner is that they can stay true to who they are as they expand. BlogHer saw that they needed to find a bigger pond, but they refused to sell out, just up. SheKnows allows them to build authentically across more media platforms and keep paying their community more. They will expand but not compromise as they find new spaces and new countries to connect women in and never forget: Maintaining integrity is essential no matter how you grow.

> *You can't get bigger and delude yourself; you can't get bigger and dilute yourself.*

In other words, remain true to who you are and own that story no matter how you choose to grow. I am always who I am. Even when I'm an ass and have to apologize, I'm just being me. Heck, I'm human. We all are—or should be. Because even when I am an ass, I will always be *this* ass, not adopting or adapting anyone else's.

LESSONS LEARNED: FIND A BIGGER POND

There is always somebody bigger than you or getting bigger and gaining. Even Henry Ford learned this the hard way. He thought big, acted bigger, and became one of the biggest businessmen in America. But Ford lost his battle to make ethanol a fuel option for his Model Ts because he ran afoul of someone even more powerful: John D. Rockefeller and the oil industry he once monopolized, which sought to rule the auto fuel industry with gasoline. Still, no one accuses Henry Ford of playing small ball. He tried to innovate and do what he needed to do by asking, "What's next?" Always ask, "What's next?" and then find bigger ponds to grow or sustain your business.

> *Adapt*: Re-envision the pond by proactively changing what you are doing now while you are successful and making sure your people and customers are aligned around that change.
> *Ask*: Listen to what your customers are telling you as you consider expanding into new markets—does your value or value proposition translate?
> *Automate and systematize*: Make your pond faster with communication, automation, and systematization so that you make better use of the resources you have.

In the end, what's next must be about more than money. All the ideas in this chapter and indeed the entire book are about ownership, not money. A quick return on investment of time and venture capital? I'm not about that. I invest everything I am in what I do. That's how I stay authentic! You can't get bigger and delude yourself; you can't get bigger and dilute yourself.

CHAPTER TEN

REACH OUT AND TOUCH SOMEONE

Have a Servant Mentality

W hen was the last time you sent someone a purple terrycloth bathrobe?

Yes, I'm serious. Let me explain why.

I am not rich. I am not a superstar. I was not born with a silver spoon in my mouth. I did not get where I am because I am smarter or always physically or fiscally bigger than my competition. I have thought big and acted bigger in everything I do, but I have not done it and cannot do it on my own. I got where I am in part because somebody mentored me, gave me advice, or guided me when I needed help. Thus, to think big and act bigger and move forward in the most open-hearted way, I never forget to pay it forward relentlessly in the smallest, most intimate way possible: helping others.

Why do I do so much for others? *They asked, and someone did it for me.* Those people who helped me knew what I have now learned myself: We get ahead by helping others get ahead, too. The more I help people, the more it comes back to me in some way. Don't lose sight of that, *ever.*

> *If you need help, ask. If someone asks, answer.*

Simply put, people serve people, not companies. That's the key to the undervalued leadership component of likeability: a genuine "servant mentality." When steamrolling obstacles, searching for the unknown, and finding bigger ponds, leaders and their businesses can achieve incredible momentum, but that momentum can also blind us to the importance of relationships in defining who we are. No matter what the Supreme Court says, companies are not people; companies are what people make them. This goes well beyond serving the needs of our customers; leaders must be willing at any time to ask anyone they connect to:

➤ How can I help you?
➤ What can I help you with?
➤ What can I do?

We must never let momentum, lack of time, success, ego, or any other excuse keep us from asking those questions. We must be relentlessly thoughtful and aware, always asking, "How am I serving others?" Note: I am *not* talking about being nice or even playing nice. You can be nice and still be completely self-serving and oblivious. To be thoughtful and aware doesn't require niceness, money, or power; only that we pay attention, genuinely want to connect with others, and aren't resentful that we need to be that way.

Sound easy? Then why do so many companies and leaders fail at the simplest of activities: customer service? Why pretend to prefer customers if you can't take the time to talk to them? Don't hide behind online submission forms, emails that go nowhere, and endless phone trees that never reach a representative. Why do so many of us find it so hard to remember a birthday, anniversary, or just an opportunity to pay forward a kindness? And what happens when we remember that we forgot? We get angry with ourselves and offer seemingly-heartfelt-but-really-I'm-just-making-an-excuse-for-not-doing-something-so-it's-about-me-not-you "I'm sorrys." No one wants to hear that. How do you feel when someone says, "I'm sorry" like that? Do you find it genuine? I find it makes me feel worse. Don't worry, I get it; you were too busy doing something else to remember me.

Which brings me back to that super-soft purple terrycloth bathrobe. I sent it to a client on his birthday. He loves purple and going to spas. Why? *Because I can.* And I should. That is what is important. Were you expecting something more? It doesn't need to be big or expensive to mean much, just thoughtful. I have a business partner from Calgary who, like most Canadians, thinks the world revolves around hockey. He has a teenage son who thinks exactly the same, so I sent them a personalized autographed copy of *The Code*, a hockey book by Ross Bernstein, whom I happen to know. They were as surprised and grateful as my writer Jim was when I sent his bacon-loving family an unexpected shipment of my favorite slices from Nueske's Applewood Smoked Meats. Those are some of the small ways I have taken care of people with no other reason than because I can and should.

Thus, we come to the last dance of balancing acts in this book, and it takes us back to where we started: A "because I can" attitude must be a blend of selfish and selfless.

My business partners are constantly annoyed by how over and above I go to try to help people—

> *Be both selfish and selfless every single day.*

from my willingness to write *another* recommendation to pro-bono consulting. I admit I can get a bit lost in it. I recently met with a small, low-six-figure business for an entire afternoon because I liked them and wanted them to be successful. I could have spent that same afternoon with a business that had three or four more zeroes at the end of its annual revenue sheet and been paid for it. I do have to remember I have only so much time in the day. My partners are trying to protect me from being my own worst enemy. But I love helping people. Maybe at times I am my own *best* enemy when I let it distract me or get carried away. Mostly I just believe it is for everyone's benefit.

You never know, there might be a pony in there.

ASK AND YE SHALL RECEIVE: THE PROMISE (AND PITFALLS) OF PONIES

A Verizon Wireless commercial from 2007 pokes fun at the idea that a pony is the best present and friend a little girl can have. Three teenage girls stand shivering in a backyard after Christmas. Looking toward the back fence, one girl says to the friend whose house it is, "You actually got a pony." The friend, not looking the least bit like she is living a fantasy, rolls her eyes and jealously eyes the phones her friends got from their parents. Cut to the pony, viciously chewing off the top of a doghouse and angrily neighing and spitting, startling the girls. "Does he bite?" the friends ask. "Yeah," their friend replies, unamused.

As a cowboy at heart, I'm not sure why anyone wouldn't want a pony; I see promise even in one that bites and spits. As a businessman, I feel the same way. Even when faced with people or situations as figuratively annoying, loud, and unpleasant as that girl's pony, I might find myself helping, working with, or engaging them, because I believe something good might come from it. I know I am an eternal optimist in thinking this way. At times I'm wrong, but I feel better thinking like Jim Carrey's character in *Dumb and Dumber*. When a beautiful girl tells him there's a one in a million chance they could be together, he thinks, "There's a chance. YEAH!"

I will serve anyone any time I can, because I can.

I like being hopeful. Even in the worst encounters, there might be a pony in there somewhere! Why would you want to kill off that hope? That innocence? I may make a mistake once. I might fight through a lousy book that never got better after the first page, but if there's no pony inside, I won't make that mistake again. And if I do find a pony? I know what to look for faster and better next time. I might even learn something in the negative: that this book and this author are something I never want to emulate.

When it comes to people, though, how do you stop yourself from getting taken advantage of with this attitude? You don't! Well, not completely. It is going to happen. Did you do it for the right reasons? Okay. Did the people you helped? If they didn't, shame on them. There's a fine line between generosity and idiocy, for sure. You just have to learn to patrol that line and have people who stop you when you can't see someone is taking advantage of your generosity. That said, my partners also understand that talking to people seeking help or advice strengthens my belief in what I am doing and my ability to think big and act bigger.

By all means, remember to keep your BS meter up for people asking for money for nothing, making promises they cannot deliver, who are meandering and directionless, who start conversations that go nowhere, or who "just want to pick your brain" instead of paying for that access and expertise. I have no tolerance for laziness, and I am careful not to let in Trojan horses while looking out for ponies. There *are* a lot of users in this world. Takers are going to take.

I prefer to define myself against the takers. I prefer to ask, "What are the consequences of not doing all I can and more?" People want to be around people who give, and there are plenty of opportunities to give back in business, from mentoring to supporting charities with more than just a check to working with students to being an active member of your community. Random acts of kindness are always appreciated, but what you plan to do says even more. That requires thoughtfulness.

And if the things I just mentioned are too much for you, just commit to doing the simplest things I do:

- ➤ Email or message me directly, and I will respond as soon as I can.
- ➤ Follow me on Twitter, and I will follow you back.
- ➤ Ask me for something, and I will do it, try, or at least tell you why I can't.
- ➤ Invite me to something, and I will be grateful, even if I can't come.

➤ Send me bacon, and I will never, ever forget you—even if my wife tells me we can't be friends anymore.

How many people do you find who won't do these things? I'm not saying this is my purpose in life. My purpose is to build wealth for my family, learn, and have fun, but I don't need to be an asshole along the way. Who won't answer an email? Are you kidding me? What happens when you or someone you touch doesn't touch back? How does it make *you* feel? Why would you want to make someone else feel that way?

Most important, why would you expect people to connect with and help you when you reach out and say hello? And I will. Don't be surprised after you ask me for something if I ask for something back. Some of my ponies will help me ride to bigger successes in the future. Some will be riding right beside me as I do.

> I am not going to be the person who is going to have the funeral home call Rent-a-Pallbearer. Who will be at your funeral?

I understand we are all busy, but I find those who at least try to have a servant mentality are the ones I remember and stay in touch with. Pick up the phone and call one of those people right now. You'll be surprised how happy they are to hear from you. Even in an age when we are so wired and connected, we are surprisingly disconnected from each other. Remedy that. If Matt Preschern, executive vice president and CMO of the multibillion-dollar Indian global IT services company HCL Technologies, can acknowledge every email he gets within 24 hours, what's your excuse? "Anyone can reach me on my globally enabled phone any time of day, and I enjoy it," he says. "I am genuinely enthusiastic about serving my team, because my and our success is dependent on them. You have to have this authentic level of enjoyment in everything you do for them." My friend Russ Mann, the former CEO of Covario and current CMO of Nintex, makes a point of going through his LinkedIn and reaching out to reconnect with people he knows in the cities he travels to (even if he hasn't seen them in years): "It's amazing how many of them write back and say, 'I really appreciate your being in touch,'" he says. "They now know I am thinking about them, and I refuse to delegate that. Even if they are not pertinent for my current job, it's always great to connect and keep the network fresh. People seem to think it is remarkable, but it's a natural part of my personal workflow."

Even in the age of social media, it's remarkable? Wow, that's how bad most of us are at it.

In the end, I'm a big believer in karma, which is Sanskrit for "action" and usually means our fate is the result of our actions. The Native Americans of South Dakota where I come from believed in something similar. What it really comes down to is ethics, accountability, and responsibility to something bigger than we are, and to me, there is nothing bigger in business than the people we work with.

A SERVANT SERVES OTHERS

In his book *Waiter Rant*, Steve Dublanica offers "40 Tips on How to Be a Good Customer." Tip number 40 is: "If you can't afford to leave a tip, you can't afford to eat in the restaurant. Stay home." I say something similar when it comes to having a servant mentality with your people:

If you can't afford to serve your people, you don't deserve to have them in your business. Get out.

This hearkens back to my saying in Chapter 1 that I want to beat the living crap out of everyone who has beaten down young people, especially young women, instead of pushing them to be bigger than they are. I hate to watch people miss out because of voices in their heads that say they can't do it. The fault is ours as leaders. No matter where you go or what you do, you need to cherish the people you love and work with.

> *Serve others, and they will serve you back.*

Say what you will about Hillary Clinton, it does take a village—not only devout followers, but also leaders devoted to them. That's the hallmark of great entrepreneurs and businesses that have moved past the devout follower stage and hired skilled technicians and professionals to gain scale. That scale will crush leaders who aren't devoted to their employees, right down to the ones who greet you at the front desk and take your messages. Chances are, those are the people who will be there when you get crushed.

That's what happened to Dave Pottruck at Charles Schwab on July 19, 2004. Dave had spent two decades at the company, rising all the way to CEO. He had built a legendary corporate culture that made Charles Schwab a great place to work. But the first dotcom bubble had taken its toll and Charles Schwab had yet to recover. Layoffs were the norm, and the stock price languished. Charles Schwab's board of directors blamed Dave and asked him to step down in favor of Charles Schwab returning to the CEO position.

It says a lot about Dave that Charles Schwab delivered the message himself. It says more about Dave when you consider what happened after that. After Dave checked in at home and received support from his wife, Emily, and then got ahold of his longtime leadership coach, Terry Pearce, the next person he called was his assistant of 15 years, Colleen Bagan-McGill, who was in the car with her family on her way to vacation. What happened then says most of all: Instead of taking her vacation, Colleen returned to the office and quit. She was the big earner in her family, but to her it did not matter. If Dave was going, she was going. She knew he would be successful and would take care of her, and until that time she would take care of him. He went from private jets and chauffeured limousines to having Colleen pick him up in a minivan and cart them around while they looked for the next landing, her baby in the back, Cheerios on the floor.

Colleen is still with Dave to this day. When I mentioned her name as part of a word association exercise during my interview of him at my C-Suite Network Conference (http://c-suitetv.com/video/executive-perspectives-dave-pottruck/), I saw something change in his eyes. "The person who does all the real work," he answered.

Do you inspire devotion like that in the people you work with, and is the feeling mutual? If not, what can you do to change that? Ask them! Acknowledge their presence! Be aware of their existence and the stories they tell! I know what I said that day onstage when Dave was a little surprised I even knew Colleen's name: "I would like to say I know a lot, but I have good staff. I've got good people." Always have, always will.

In fact, every single business and person I have quoted in this book is included not just because they are successful, but because they believe in the power of having great people and know their importance to thinking big and acting bigger.

Our stories cannot be written without them.

LESSONS LEARNED: HAVE A SERVANT MENTALITY

People serve people, not companies, and that's the most undervalued leadership component: a genuine "servant mentality." No matter what the U.S. Supreme Court says, companies are not people; companies are what people make them. Do you know the power of even the smallest thoughtful gestures that build and maintain relationships? This goes well beyond serving the needs of our customers; leaders must be willing at any time to perform the following tasks:

- If you need help, ask. If someone asks, answer: How can I help you? What can I help you with? What can I do?
- Your "because I can" attitude must be a blend of selfish and selfless.
- Serve as many people any time you can, because you can: There might be a pony in there somewhere!
- Be ethical with, accountable to, and responsible to the people you work with: If you can't afford to serve your people, you don't deserve to have them in your business. Get out.

It really comes down to those ethics, that accountability, and our responsibility to something bigger than we are. To me, there is nothing bigger in business than the people we work with. Do you inspire devotion like that in the people you work with, and is the feeling mutual? If not, what can you do to change that? Ask them! Acknowledge their presence! Be aware of their existence and the stories they tell!

GET OFF YOUR ASS and MAKE IT HAPPEN!

received the Frost & Sullivan Lifetime Achievement Award for marketing when I was in my mid-40s, and while I was honored, I remember thinking, "Holy crap! It's *over* for me?!" I have since been named to halls of fame and received other career awards, but I am not an athlete. I am not done with my playing career, ready to hang it up and watch someone else do what I once did. I have many more games to play on many different fields. More books to write, shows to create, networks to grow, grandchildren to take for a ride on my tractor (as soon as I get a tractor), and other things I can't even imagine right now. I have a bucket list that will never be filled.

I appreciate the honors, but I still have a ways to go. That's why when people ask me, "What's the best thing you have ever done?" I say, "I don't know. I haven't done it yet!"

What defines us is our next thing: the next promise we make and keep, because a brand is nothing more than a promise delivered. Forget what you have done, and make the next thing happen. Does this contradict what I said before about never forgetting? No! Acknowledge and appreciate success, but don't let what you have done define what is next for you. *Never* forget the lessons in this book, what you have learned and where you come from. But never rest on what you have done. Celebrate it and move on—be willing to let go, start over, and be a beginner again. Own something new as a bigger, better, and badder you!

I can't conceive of a time I will stop thinking big and acting bigger. Sure, I have an end game in play for what I am doing and building now—and I know my conditions of satisfaction for what I do in my life—but I don't know exactly where it is going to take me. I just know that I am going to be good at what I do when I get there. I know I am eventually going to win again *because I can make it happen, and you can, too.*

> *Remember:*
> *Something is*
> *only impossible*
> *because you*
> *think it is!*

Ken Kragen, who created and organized historic humanitarian events including "We Are the World" and Hands Across America, told me a story that perfectly sums up what often stands in the way of accomplishing the seemingly impossible. In the 1950s, he worked for a summer at North American Aviation, which milled metal for airplane wings as thin as 1/1,000 of an inch. Then an order came in with a requirement that the metal be milled to 1/10,000 of an inch—ten times thinner. It had never been done before. North American went to its millers and asked them to do it, and their best millers told them it was impossible. Sure enough, they all failed. They tried extra training, and still no one could do it. Finally, the company hired a few skilled technicians from other industries who had never done milling before, trained them on the machines, and told them to mill the metal to 1/10,000 of an inch, never telling them its millers had failed or that it had never been done.

They did it. Because they didn't know it could not be done. They had no stories in their heads telling them it was impossible before they even got started. We believe so much is impossible—that so many things will not work, cannot work, or simply cannot be done in a certain way. We are thinking small, so we act smaller.

Thus, we have come full circle. There is only one thing left to do: Do it! Or, to go back to my cowboy roots one last time, saddle up and RIDE! Nobody's going to do the thinking for you or act on your behalf. No one is even thinking about you most of the time. It's time for you to get off your literal and figurative ass and relentlessly create and own some powerful new stories about who you are and what is possible, focus hard on what matters to make those stories come to life, and make it happen by steamrolling the obstacles in front of you.

I know you can do it, because you can.

PEOPLE AND COMPANIES CONSULTED
(Alphabetical by Name)

Carl Bass, Chief Executive Officer, Autodesk (www.autodesk.com)

Bennet James Bayer, former Global Chief Marketing Officer, Huawei Technologies

Walter Bond, Walter Bond Seminars Inc. (www.walterbond.com)

LeVar Burton, Curator-in-Chief, RRKidz Inc. (www.readingrainbow.com)

Cadillac (www.cadillac.com)

Paul Carbone, Chief Financial Officer, Dunkin' Brands (www.dunkinbrands.com)

Jory Des Jardins, President, Global Strategic Alliances, BlogHer (www.blogher.com)

Domino's Pizza (www.dominos.com)

Peter Friedman, Chairman and Chief Executive Officer, LiveWorld (www.liveworld.com)

Greg Glassman, Chief Executive Officer, CrossFit (www.crossfit.com)

Jermaine Griggs, Founder, Hear and Play Music and AutomationClinic.com (www.jermainegriggs.com)

Bonnie Harvey and Michael Houlihan, co-founders, Barefoot Wine, international business keynote speakers, and corporate trainers (www.thebarefootspirit.com)

Scott Jordan, Chief Executive Officer, SCOTTeVEST Inc. (www.scottevest.com)

Brendan King, Chief Executive Officer, Vendasta Technologies (www.vendasta.com)

Ken Kragen, author, producer, and organizer of humanitarian events (www.kenkragen.com)

Matthew Lanfear, Chief Executive Officer, Great Eastern Energy (www.greateasternenergy.com)

Glenn Llopis, President and Chief Executive Officer, Glenn Llopis Group (www.glennllopis.com)

Heidi Lorenzen, former Chief Marketing Officer and executive in several Silicon Valley startups and large tech companies

Don Lowe, Chief Executive Officer, Franchise Services, Inc. (www.franserv.com)

Richard Lowe, President and Chief Operating Officer, Franchise Services, Inc. (www.franserv.com)

Greg Lucier, former Chief Executive Officer, Life Technologies (www.life technologies.com)

Russ Mann, Chief Marketing Officer, Nintex (www.nintex.com)

David L. Meinz, Director, Executive Heart Program (www.executiveheartprogram.com)

Elisa Camahort Page, Chief Operating Officer, BlogHer (www.blogher.com)

Peter Philippi, Chief Executive Officer, Strategex (www.strategex.com)

Dave Pottruck, Chairman, Red Eagle Ventures (www.redeagleventures.com)

Matt Preschern, Executive Vice President and Chief Marketing Officer, HCL Technologies (www.hcltech.com)

Eddie Rausch, Chief Operating Officer and Chairman, Veteran Tickets Foundation (www.vettix.org)

The Seattle Sounders (www.soundersfc.com)

Deidre Siegel, Chief Executive Officer, PEAR Core Solutions Inc. (www.pearcoresolutions.com)

Gene Simmons, KISS, founder, entrepreneur, and television personality (www.genesimmons.com)

Lisa Stone, Chief Executive Officer, BlogHer (www.blogher.com)

Jaycen Thorgeirson, Chief Executive Officer, UviaUs (www.uviaus.com)

Michael Williams, former Chief Marketing Officer, Grand Prix America

Jeff Winsper, President, Winsper and Black Ink (www.winsper.com)

Mark Wolfe, Chief Executive Officer, RRKidz Inc. (www.readingrainbow.com)

Tania Yuki, Chief Executive Officer, Shareablee (www.shareablee.com)

ACKNOWLEDGMENTS

B IGGEST thanks to:

Jim Eber, who captures my thoughts and ramblings and turns them into something that makes me bigger than necessary.

Wendy Keller, my agent, who makes me money but who was and is my friend first.

Linda Maschino, my executive assistant, who keeps me on track even though I always make it difficult.

Tyler Hayzlett, who runs the business of me better than I do.

Lindsey Hayzlett, for protecting her papa and whose own success will be bigger than anything I ever do.

Tami Hayzlett, for allowing me to be me and act like I am the one in charge.

Karl Post, for being the master of details and deliverer of the things we do so well.

The TallGrass and C-Suite Network teams for ACTING BIGGER.

The people and companies who contributed their words and stories to make this book the BIGGEST book it could be.

Jillian McTigue (benevolent overseer of all), Jen Dorsey (editor extraordinaire), Karen Billipp (brilliant production manager), and Vanessa Campos (keeper of marketing) at Entrepreneur for their wonderful partnership in creating something BIG.

Frontier Bank, for being a great partner in making us BIGGER.

My horses: It's time to ride.

Bacon, because, well, hell, it's bacon! (Bacon lovers, even if you prefer the vegan kind, tell everyone else to shut up; they'll never understand.)

All those who came before me: I am a product of you; thank you for the time of my life. It's sometimes hard but worth it.

And to my readers, viewers, fans, and friends: for your engagement and encouragement—you make it worth it!

ABOUT THE AUTHOR

J effrey Hayzlett is a global business celebrity; prime-time television and radio show host; bestselling author; sought-after keynote speaker; and sometime cowboy. From small businesses to international corporations, he puts his creativity and extraordinary entrepreneurial skills into play, launching ventures blending his leadership perspectives, insights into professional development, mass marketing prowess, and affinity for social media.

Jeffrey is a leading business expert, cited in *Forbes*, *SUCCESS*, Mashable, *Marketing Week,* and *Chief Executive*, among many others. He shares his executive insight and commentary on television networks like

Bloomberg, MSNBC, Fox Business, and C-Suite TV. Jeffrey is a former Bloomberg contributing editor and prime-time host, and has appeared as a guest celebrity judge on NBC's *The Celebrity Apprentice with Donald Trump* for three seasons.

Jeffrey hosts *C-Suite with Jeffrey Hayzlett* and *Executive Perspectives* on C-Suite TV. On *C-Suite with Jeffrey Hayzlett*, Jeffrey takes viewers inside the C-Suite of some of the world's biggest companies. He asks the tough questions to get to the bottom of business, and discovers what makes C-level executives tick. On *Executive Perspectives*, Jeffrey interviews business executives, thought leaders, and innovators live on stage, with interviews being recorded in front of live audiences. He brings viewers a front-row seat to some of the most interesting and innovating game changers in business today. Jeffrey is also the host of *All Business with Jeffrey Hayzlett*, which airs on CBS on-demand radio network Play.It and C-Suite Radio. Jeffrey goes inside the good, bad, and ugly of recent business results from some of today's biggest headline makers.

Jeffrey is the author of two previous business bestsellers, *Running the Gauntlet: Essential Business Lessons to Lead, Drive Change and Grow Profits* and *The Mirror Test: Is Your Business Really Breathing*. *The Mirror Test* received acclaim on numerous bestseller lists including 800 CEO Read, *The Wall Street Journal*, and *USA Today*.

Jeffrey has years of international marketing, sales, and customer relations management experience. In 2010, Jeffrey stepped down from his role of Chief Marketing Officer at Eastman Kodak Company, where he was responsible for Brand Development and Management, Market Development, Corporate and Product Public Relations, Communications and Public Affairs, Corporate Sponsorships, Business Development, Corporate Relationships and Partnerships, and Marketing. Prior to joining Kodak, he led a private business development and public relations firm specializing in the technology and visual communications industries. He also held senior management positions in strategic business development and marketing at several companies, including Cenveo, Webprint, and Colorbus, Inc., and served in staff positions in the United States Senate and House of Representatives.

Throughout his career, Jeffrey has received numerous global marketing and business awards and served in prestigious organizations. In 2015, he was elected to the National Speakers Association Hall of Fame. He currently leads The Hayzlett Group and is Chairman of TallGrass Public Relations, offering strategic business, marketing, and PR consulting, leading change for high growth businesses globally. He is also Co-Founder and Chairman of C-Suite Network, the most powerful network of C-Suite leaders. Drawing upon an eclectic background in business, buoyed by a stellar track record of keynote speaking, and deeply rooted in cowboy lore, Jeffrey energizes his role driving and delivering change. He is a turnaround architect of the highest order, a maverick marketer who delivers scalable campaigns, embraces traditional modes of customer engagement, and possesses a remarkable cachet of mentorship, corporate governance, and brand building. Even when away from his home state of South Dakota, Jeffrey can always be found in his trademark cowboy boots. Learn more at www.hayzlett.com.

index

A

Abercrombie & Fitch, 85–86

actions, owning, 19–20, 39–44. *See also* Katelyn Rule

adapting, 135–139, 149

admitting failure, 119–127

"and", power of, 103–105

asking the right questions, 23, 142

authenticity, 72–75, 123, 134, 140

Autodesk, 104–105

automation, 143–146, 149

awareness

    admitting failure and, 119–124

    brand awareness, 124–127

    of customer needs, 121–126, 139–145, 149

    of employee needs, 88–89, 122

    maintaining, 115–116, 127–130

    tunnel vision and, 113–115, 129–130

    of what you don't know, 116–119

B

Bagan-McGill, Colleen, 158

balance, 135–136

Barefoot Wine, 28–29, 83–84

bathroom, cleaning your own, 77–81

"because I can" attitude, xi–xii, 6, 10–12, 31–32, 153–154

being yourself, 3–12, 31–32, 44. *See also* transparency

bigger ponds, 133–135, 149
BlogHer, 147–148
brand awareness, 124–127
Burton, LeVar, 95–98

C

cadence, 67–76, 78, 126
Cadillac, 124–127
Charles Schwab, 37–38, 158
cleaning your own bathroom,
    77–81
conditions of satisfaction, 9,
    11–12
connecting with your business,
    75, 77–83, 88, 91–92. *See also*
    disconnection
contradictory thoughts, 44
core self, 3–12, 31–32, 44. *See also*
    transparency
Covario, 103–104
CrossFit, 69–71
crowdfunding, 97–98
culture, 68–69, 73–76. *See also*
    cadence
customers, 60–61, 121–126, 139–
    145, 149
cutting-edge thinking, 34–38,
    44–45. *See also* unconventional
    thinking

D

disconnection, 78, 83–87, 90–91.
    See also connecting with your
    business
disruptive innovations, 118–119
distractions, 49–55
Domino's Pizza, 119–124
Dunkin' Donuts, 71
Dyson, James, 72–73

E

80/20 Rule, 56–57

emotional attachments, 60–61
employees
    empowering, 12–18, 62–64, 65, 90
    firing, 60
    listening to, 88–89, 122
    systems and, 72–76
enemies, 107–111
excuses, 39–45, 57–61, 65

F

FailCon, 21
failure, 20–25, 28, 119–127
focus
    "can't focus" problem, 57–59
    distractions and, 49–55
    "don't want to focus" problem,
        59–61
    emotional attachments and,
        60–61
    excuses for not focusing, 57–61,
        65
    important vs. unimportant tasks
        and, 52–54
    maintaining, 50–55, 64–65
    Millennials and, 61, 68
    Pareto Principle and, 56–57
    team focus, 62–64, 65
    time management and, 52–55
focus triangles, 52–55
Ford, Henry, 131–133
franchise owners, 16–17
funding, 96–98

G

giving back, 151–155
golden screw (joke), 11
Great Eastern Energy (GEE), 73
Griggs, Jermaine, 143–146
groundedness, 86, 89, 91–92

H

HCL Technologies, 89–90

HearandPlay.com, 143–145
helping others, 151–159
honesty, 123–124. *See also* transparency
hooks, 10
hopefulness, 154–155
hubris, 118–119

I

important vs. unimportant tasks, 52–54
irrational leadership, 34–38, 44–45. *See also* unconventional thinking

J

Johnny Vegas Syndrome, 79

K

Katelyn Rule, 12–17
Kickstarter, 97–98
KISS, 26–27
knowing what you don't know, 116–119

L

Life Technologies, 35–36
likeability, 152
listening, 88–89, 121–126, 139–145, 149
losing, 20–22. *See also* failure
Lucier, Greg, 35–36
Lululemon, 86–87

M

Market Basket, 88–89
Millennials, 61, 68
mistakes, owning, 19–20
modesty, 11
mood shifting, 126, 130

N

next thing, 133–135, 149, 161–163

"no one is going to die" attitude, 19–21, 28
North American Aviation, 162–163
no-win scenarios, 21. *See also* failure

O

obstacles
    enemies and, 107–111
    steamrolling, 95–97
    traditional thinking as, 98–99
    unconventional thinking and, 99–107
offending people, 39–40
optimism, 154–155
organizational culture, 68–69, 73–76. *See also* cadence
outside-the-box thinking, 99–100. *See also* unconventional thinking
ownership, 6–12, 17–20, 39–44. *See also* Katelyn Rule

P

Pareto Principle, 56–57
passion, 25–29
paying forward, 151–155
perfection, 20–21
perspective, 87–92, 115–116
Philippi, Peter, 56–57
pigheadedness, 31–34. *See also* pushing hard
pitches, 9–10, 82–83
Pottruck, Dave, 37–38, 158
print businesses, 137–138
purposeful desperation, 107
pushing hard, 44–45. *See also* pigheadedness

R

rationalizations, 39. *See also* excuses
reaching out, 154–157
Reading Rainbow, 95–98
relationships, 89–90

resiliency, 105–107
risk taking, 119–121, 122
rivalries, 108–109
Rockefeller, John D., 132–133
RRKidz Inc., 95–98

S
satisfaction, 9, 11–12
SCOTTeVEST Inc., 105–108
Seattle Seahawks, 100–101
Seattle Sounders, 99–103
selling, 9–10
selling up, 146–149
servant mentality, 152, 156–159
serving others, 151–159
Shark Tank (TV show), 90–91, 107–108
SheKnows Media, 148
Simmons, Gene, 26–27
small thinking, vii–viii, 81–82, 162–163. *See also* thinking
Sounders, 99–103
stories, 6–12, 17–18
stretching, 133–135
success, 22
systems, 67–69, 72–76, 143–146, 149

T
target markets, 139–143
team focus, 62–64, 65
TED (Technology, Entertainment, Design) Talks, 6–7
Thank you, Captain Obvious (TYCO), 63–64
thinking. *See also* irrational leadership
  big, 81–83, 97

outside-the-box, 99–100
small, ix–x, 81–82, 162–163
traditional, 98–99
unconventional, 99–107, 162–163
time management, 52–55
traditional thinking, 98–99. *See also* thinking
transparency, 5, 121, 123–124. *See also* true self
true self, 3–12, 31–32, 44. *See also* transparency
tunnel vision, 113–115, 129–130
TYCO (Thank you, Captain Obvious), 63–64

U
unconventional thinking, 99–107, 162–163. *See also* irrational leadership; thinking
unknown unknowns, 116, 118–119
UviaUs, 138–139

V
Vendasta Technologies, 36
visibility, 81
visual communications businesses, 138–139

W
what's next, asking yourself, 133–135, 149, 161–163
willingness to act, 22
winning, 22, 133
win-win scenarios, 21
Wolfe, Mark, 95–98